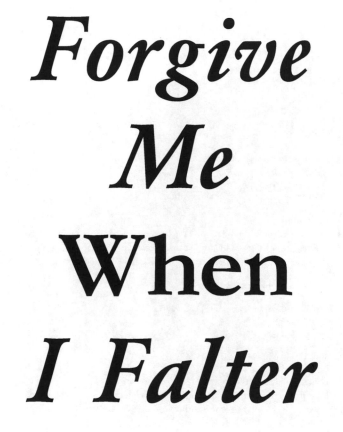

*Forgive
Me
When
I Falter*

Order this book online at www.trafford.com
or email orders@trafford.com

Most Trafford titles are also available at major online book retailers.

Printed in the United States of America.

ISBN: 978-1-4907-4025-6 (sc)
ISBN: 978-1-4907-4026-3 (hc)
ISBN: 978-1-4907-4027-0 (e)

Library of Congress Control Number: 2014911269

Because of the dynamic nature of the Internet, any web addresses or links contained in
this book may have changed since publication and may no longer be valid. The views
expressed in this work are solely those of the author and do not necessarily reflect the
views of the publisher, and the publisher hereby disclaims any responsibility for them.

Any people depicted in stock imagery provided by Thinkstock are models,
and such images are being used for illustrative purposes only.
Certain stock imagery © Thinkstock.

Trafford rev. 06/23/2014

www.trafford.com

North America & international
toll-free: 1 888 232 4444 (USA & Canada)
fax: 812 355 4082

Also by Phillip D. Reisner

Whispering
Time Remnants
Letters to Angela
I See Movies In My Head
Dichotomy

Preface

Most everyone abandons ship when someone or something fails and circumstances disappoint expectations. I wish to poetically look at a few failings and near failings in order to shed some light on the why, when and how of failure. I see failure as something rather dramatic that many times has consequences far beyond the initial happenstance. I am somewhat concerned with human failure at this point in our discussion. I could go into mechanical, chemical, electrical, etc. failure, but that would be more like engineering rather than humanitarian circumstances. I am not so concerned with individual or private failure or even mutual or societal failure. In fact, I am concerned with personal faltering rather than failure.

Faltering is common and happens more frequently than failing. Faltering is a wavering or hesitating condition that precludes failure and sometimes even prevents failure. Faltering is not always bad. It is usually when little problems surface before a big problem happens. It seems like little things drive people crazy while big things tend to defy sanity. People get together because they have a few big things in common. Sometimes big problems bring people together while often little problems break them apart. Big things become personal soon after people get together and tend to unite them like a family merging. It is later that little, everyday common things become problems. Things like job, career and children are big things that bond people. Things like toothpaste squeezing and bed sheet kicking separate people.

I cannot express well in ordinary terms my concern for all sizes of breakdowns and malfunctions that frequently cause people to often falter and sometimes fail. I hope to delve into many subjects with a few words that make sense to the reader. I have written about failure previously and will touch on it a little bit here—faltering is my main theme in this book—and I will keep my focus on the preventive assessment side of life.

It seems nearly all circumstances carry about the same weight except for a few things like war and peace, life and death, cancer and heart attack, and heaven and hell. Now those are heavy-duty, deadly situations. It seems most people can ponder and laugh about most things, believing that they are not worth crying or fighting about. I chose to have few principles and thus little about which to fight. I say, "have few principles" because you might have to go to war over them. Faltering and possibly failing over principles is usually not pretty and can be occasionally deadly.

I begin writing in this book about the mind, then move to the heart, and conclude with the soul. I think conflicts between heavenly spirit and earthly body cause big faltering concerns and enormous failure fears.

People are like flowers that need nurturing throughout life—each person wishes to be a beautiful blossoming plant that everyone recognizes and admires. Some of us are seemingly weeds very early in life while others are wonderful flowers at birth. It is kind of luck of the draw I guess. I believe, however, that we are not helpless to change discovered circumstances and that we can transform perceived weeds into flowers. A person must be constantly aware of their strengths and weaknesses—and the environment in which they find themselves—thus they become attentive to faltering and failing possibilities. Each person should attempt to modify life circumstances at the faltering stage and not the failing stage. With God's help, it is never too late to change.

The definition of faltering is to hesitate, pause or waver from some course of action. I believe that many people disappoint and cause inconvenience or hardship to others. Expectation many times becomes a negative experiential event. Anticipation is usually a positive state of mind that causes degrees of hope and fulfillment. I am personally better off anticipating waking in the morning rather than expecting to wake. So far, I have not been disappointed, thanks to God.

I anticipate going to heaven. On what solid ground can I place my reasoning for going to heaven you ask? My fragile anticipation is based on belief in Jesus. I think my whole life is probably like balancing on the head of a mystical needle, while an angel occasionally helps stability, I anticipate direction of mind, body and spirit. In the final analysis, I must have intelligence enough to expect death on Earth and faith enough to anticipate eternal life in heaven.

I think the whole existence experience is a balancing act of finding middle ground between positive and negative circumstances. It certainly is a blessing to find the positive side of existence. There are many places in the world where mostly negative circumstances exist. I think the United States is the most positive place in the world and I thank God every day for having been born here. My parents were a blessing and I am presently blessed. I have had only one horrible negative experience in my life. After one suffers the worst possible loss, everything else is a piece of cake. We eat little pieces of cake during our lives if we are lucky. Sometimes the cake is not so good and sometimes it is delicious.

I only hope that my mind is sound and well enough when I die that I can experience the returning home event. It will be a once in a life time experience and I don't want to miss any aspect of it. That is not to say that I might not have another lifetime to experience. I just might come back repeatedly until I get it right. I suspect there are previous lifetime foundation parts on which I am building an improved life.

So bear with me while I travel back and forth, side to side and up and down through my life experience to hopefully share a little wisdom. Forgive me if I am not so articulate and wise. Forgive me if I falter.

Contents

Chapter IV – Swaying Dreams 87

Chapter V – Abating Courage 115

Chapter XI – Wavering Legacy 297

Introduction

I used to ask myself where the mind is and usually came up with no good answer, but lately I have been reasoning that the mind utilizes thought, will, perception, imagination and memory. All conscious and subconscious applications are remembered processes that take place in the brain and the body.

I believe that my spirit, the real Phillip Reisner, lives within me. Memory is what created me in the first place and sustains me every day. I have in each body cell the memory to create a whole being, therefore, I propose that mind is not in my head like previously guessed, but in every cell of my body. Each cell no matter where it is located in the body works together with all other cells to provide mind.

I was born with more knowledge than can be acquired during a lifetime. I could not learn to grow and repair my body without heavenly memory. I teach my brain and body new things and provide myself with additional information to remember, but the bulk of my knowledge comes from heaven in one mysterious way or another.

The brain might be the originator of mental activities, but it is the earthly body that applies thinking, reasoning and knowledge. A body can subconsciously sustain itself up to a point, but then it must consciously continue itself through recalled knowledge. It must maintain itself with that illusive thing called memory stored in that illusive place called mind. Memory is stored in every cell of the human body. I postulate that Human consciousness begins in the brain and after a human being becomes aware of itself fifty-eight days after conception, then consciously learn how to live in a given environment.

My spirit, intelligence and perception of reality rely on what I learn and what I can remember learning. I can only speculate about the existence of my beautiful, elusive mind that propels me magnificently—through time and space with little knowledge of its power source or guidance system.

I say that my mind surely lives within me, embedded in my earthly body and overseen by my heavenly spirit. In the final analysis, I can only rely on faith to provide temporary answers, for I shall have to wait until I go to heaven for definite answers.

Chapter I

Vacillating Mind

Lingering grand thoughts
tease mind to prevail,
enlighten and make

known man's fleeting time,
while building his dreams
with mythology.

Copper Electron

I am frequently
like a disturbed
electron seeking
atom stability.
I am resolved to
eventually
find perfect
balance.
I strive to
discover own
God created
element.
I am often
life deranged.
I falter at
light speed and
flow in turmoil.
I, however,
help illuminate
existence like an
unpretentious
electron in an
affecting element.
I'm like one of
twenty-nine
enthusiastic
copper electrons
always seeking
neutrality,
afraid to wander
yet willing to
surrender.

Mind and Soul Lover

I wish to write
passionate
thoughts that
I momentarily
experience.
It seems love
flits in and
out of
my mind like a
hummingbird
intently seeking
pollen.
At least love
flits and
seeks for
only one
who bakes and
cooks,
talks and
comforts,
rubs and
massages,
kisses and
loves.
I do wish,
however, that
I could write
my passionate
thoughts that
drive me crazy.
It seems
love makes
me hungry
like a wolf,

causing an
obsession to
eat time and
energy.
For sure,
I am a
would be
emotional
thinker and
passionate
writer.
I am a
mind and
soul lover
who wishes to
make love
with brain and
body while
forgetting
all that
passionate,
romantic stuff
about which
I wish to write.

Meeting

I Stake and
Shake restaurant
entered at
exactly noon,
anxiously looked
around and
soon saw
her at my right,
fourth booth
sitting.

She was facing
me in her
straw hat with a
big smile.
I could not
believe
my eyes for
she was
prettier than
her picture.

I was surely not
disappointed
like so many
previous times.
I took
one look at
her and knew
correct decision
to meet had
been made.

Applied while
could prove
us possibly
compatible.
We ate lunch,
talked much and
soon decided
to spend more
time together
that day.

o

When push
came to
hug, and
it did,
I had
no idea of
our power.
I subtly
heard and
understood a
few words of
inner
wisdom.
I felt
privileged to
be with her.
I found
myself in a
wonderful
place to be.

Two Hours

I met my
future wife
within a small
window of
opportune
time and
recognized
her as
"the one"
in a moment.

One glance
gathered
my attention,
caused
my heart to
hope and
mind to
dream of
something
beyond self.

I was
convinced to
spend much
more time
with her
after only an
hour and
gave her a big
hug after
two hours.

Accept

Some time ago
I heard someone
speak about an
important word.
That word here on
Earth or in
heaven is
"accept."
I received an
education about
accept from
my three and a
half year old
daughter
nearly seventeen
years ago.
I have run from
that word,
been afraid of
that word and
wished it only
be placed on
me when
entering heaven.
It is surely
strange how a
moment in time,
person in midst of
change of heart
can alter a
man's attitude.
God teases
me to listen for
that word,

"accept," and
possibly hear
Him say,
"I accept you."
I pray that
I will eventually
hear Jesus say
He accepts me,
but for now,
I can only
hope to hear it
from earthlings—
spoken or
unspoken—and
especially
I wish to hear
it from a
daughter with
whom
I have not
communicated for
several years.

Seeking

I struggle
to express
passion,
feelings and
love
in life.

I seek
no greater
fulfillment
than to
know
"thyself."

I wish to
express
my human
nature as
I create
my universe.

My heart
aches,
silent soul
moans,
feeble words
evade.

My insight
falls short,
passion
stumbles,
life
now weeps.

One Word

I sought
one word to
save my soul,
a convincing
word that
celestial
spirits use
frequently.

God left
biggest
life decision
up to me,
like a simple
word brings
insight to a
lost soul.

I wished to
listen to an
angel sing,
but instead
heard a
gentle voice
whisper, "I will
accept you."

o

One word is
remarkably
leading me to
one sign,
one path and

one finale
of self
assurance.

One utterance
is restoring
me as a small
part of a
greater whole as
I ride on
shimmering
enlightenment.

I soar at
mind speed,
whispering,
"*accept* me,"
until mind and
soul are
touched and
I am home.

o

I recline
on a faithful
time bed with
cherished
memories
flowing from
my gleaming
soul suitcase.

I inner smile
for earthly
memories are
written as

musical notes on
heaven's door
to create a
known melody.

Angels further
advocate for
my obliging
canvas spirit
by painting
life events
with broad
brush strokes.

Oh, art is
superbly in
my benevolent
essence as I
eagerly listen,
aptly look and
deeply feel
heaven.

I am lighter
than air,
whiter than
snow and as
worthy made as
I can be for
I have been
accepted.

Sweet Mind State

On a grassy hill top,
sweet clover patches
abundantly grew.
Life was simple from a
child's perspective.
I walked through thick
Sugarbush trees,
climbed a long path and
watched milk cows
wandering towards my
elevated vantage point.

Now years later,
my body aches while
climbing same hill
where sweet clover yet
plentifully grows.
I lay again on an earthen
sweet clover bed,
dreaming about places
lived, visited and
called home—but now
cold soil draws body heat,
causing near hypothermia.
I dream of places that
don't steal body heat
from an old body, yet
I am compelled to
remain motionless.
I whisper, "lay me
down to sleep," but
not here at my life's
November time.

That sweet clover
covered hill waited for
my napping after
many passing years.
Life is now different
from an adult's perspective.
I have less to do and
little to wonder about as
I on grassy knoll lay—
realizing that a simple,
sweet childhood place
is always near, even if
only in my mind saying,
"welcome home."

My world was large,
when I was small.
Big trees, hills and
creeks were near a
big house on
Cuba's outskirts.
Weather threatened with
Fall accounting and
Winter punishing.
Mother Nature allowed an
impatient climate to
advance as a scary, but
graceful, phenomenon.
I traveled far and near,
found sweet clover
growing in many places, but
not so sweet as
my cool rolling hills on a
Western New York
dairy farm.

You Are Perfect

You are perfect,
flat and shiny as
could be,
like a mirror
you reflect
my six year old
face and a
blue cloudy sky
above me.
We are both small
but purposeful,
confined and
inexperienced.
Nature
deposited you
one precious
rain droplet
at a time.
You shall
same remain
until some
external force
disseminates,
splashes or
makes you shed
own tears.
But even then
you shall not
allow anything
to change
your composure.
You shall
same remain,
until you can

no longer reflect
my shiny face
with background
clouds floating.
God will soon
evaporate and
make you part of
those changing
clouds.
But until then a
shiny little
puddle is all
you are in a
world of
rivers and lakes.
At least you
are a puddle.
I am now
no more than a
single drop in an
unimaginable
human ocean.
You temporarily
fascinate and
serve my little boy
purpose for
I use you
to comb
my hair and
make silly
reflected faces.
You are more
than a reflecting
puddle to me.
You are a mirror
into my discerning
natural essence.

A Train Ride

I was a whistle-less train
rushing towards disaster
in dim morning light,
launching a weighty day as if
pulling a hundred train cars.

Distant station lights in
mindful mist grew brighter,
railroad tracks shone as
if only a wary mind could
straighten muddled steel.

There were no signs or
red warning lights.
A hundred thousand
imagined cargo tons
cruelly embraced gravity.

A little engineer voice
in bizarre, clearing mind,
then softly spoke reason,
reminding me that sunlight
always next day comes.

Unruly mind slowed and
from tracks I escaped,
realizing how anxiety
can take anyone for a
psychological train ride.

Mind Sings

Reminiscent music
floats like bitter odor
on hot summer air as
melancholy thoughts
haunt innocence and
destroy responsibility.

I secretly flounder in
depression found and
simplicity lost as
angels trade a child's
precious breath with
wilting flower odor.

Courage evades raw
inert thoughts while
I ask forgiveness for
own tearful faltering
as to Amazing Grace
Kaitlyn mind sings.

Riddle Write

If you must
riddle write
introverted
private words and
seldom speak
opinions,
then have few
principles and
allow
idealistic
words to only
flow towards
trusted ears.

Freedom
patiently seeks
success and
willingly finds
wisdom.

If you can
share direct
extroverted
free words and
write for
reliable eyes,
then deep mind
collect an
inner glow
and seek a
spiritual
influence with
honest silence.

Melding Times

Ancient ways
linger in a
mind corner,
like rain droplets
waiting for a
perfect
descending
time.

It's like wind
pushing a
thoughtful
cold front across
awareness,
where languishing
hot thick air
waits collision.

Mind
clouds gather,
growing a
tornado,
turning thoughts
around with
confounding
dilemmas.

It is like a
heavenly
insightful gate
swinging open,
like a spider
web being
precisely spun.

Knowledge
bridges eclectic
extremes as
natural balance
melds modern
desires and
ancient
wisdom.

Time has an
agenda and
assists enough
for celestial
humanity to
be placed as
earthen dust to
promulgate life.

Finally Home

I lay rotting
on an earthen
trash bed,
among patient
wild flowers,
grass and
tree sprouts,
struggling with
life awareness.

I, however,
remember
tall standing,
wind swaying and
leaf singing—and
terrifying winds
shaking my
heart and
enduring spirit.

I was
put to rest,
earth-felled with
no regrets.
I was called
"junk wood,"
something
without purpose
or usefulness.

Solace and
relief is mine
for I finally
realize that

I provided
natural beauty,
day shade and a
home for birds
and squirrels.

I am suitably
home while
sap weeping,
leaf rotting,
limb dying and
soulful heart
wood trunk
communing.

I seek
respect and
reunion as
my rotting
essence seeks
organic soil
cover and
replication.

My dank odor
earthen bed
recognizes
my name,
easily holds
me close and
accepts my
precious nature.

Mental Lowlands

Deep sadness
penetrates like
water seeping
black lowland
soil gained from
river overflow.
Containing
river banks have
no agenda,
allowing water
to meander
like a mind
wanders.
Clay and silt
is thought and
river is mind,
both need
each other for
existence.
Sadness debris
mind flows,
contaminating
hope like a
river struggling to
renew itself.
Mental lowlands
get restored by
letting sorrow
distantly flow
towards some
melancholy
receiving place,
some accepting
place.

Black muck
timely turns dry,
green and
cooperative.
It soon yields
rich flora,
likely dreams and
mended identity.
Sadness gives
more than it takes
in a natural
renewing mind.
Sorrow,
gloom and
even grief are
mending emotions
for a natural
human being.
Brief depression
is not shameful,
but necessary and
even healthy.
One must
remember that
mental lowlands
get restored by
letting sorrow
distantly flow
towards some
melancholy
concluding place.

One of Two Minds

You are a
polarized mind
traveler,
shaking earth and
uncovering
precious stones.
You seek
platforms where
extreme conflicting
drama exists,
knowing that a
narrow theater
begs naive
solutions and
pretentious
poetic justice.

You are an
oblique searcher,
disguised as a
faithful
practitioner,
building a
special church
in a cultivated
spiritual realm.
Only a monk
on a drunken
holiday
would prowl
such a mind.

Beauty arises
in shared

extremes,
like snowflakes
dusting earth
in October.

Through iron
gated gardens,
swung open
in thoughtless
haste,
your tortured
mind strolls as if
structured barriers
pose no threat.

One of two
minds can
discover more
while hiding
behind a
curtain than a
lesser one
dancing and
singing before a
watching audience.

More can be
discovered
on some dim,
narrow catwalk
with a confused,
introspective
mind than
on some bright
illuminated stage
with a mind possessing
no imagination.

Mind Weight

Heavy mind
weights
invoke
depression,
anxiety and
trepidation.

Choices weren't
available as
uncontrollable
bi-polar
thought winds
scattered logic.

Then medicine
pulled weight
from mind and
put it in a
protected,
innocent place.

Psyche then
found peace
like gathered
wheat from
thrashing and
separating.

A specified
guiding stone
rolled well,
grinding body,
mind and
soul into flour.

Wrestling

I wrestled with
perfection and
mediocrity,
liberal and
conservative,
night and
day,
sleep and
awake,
work and
play,
brilliance and
stupidity.
I further
wrestled with
fat and
skinny,
sweet and
bitter,
happiness and
sorrow,
yes and
no,
agreeing and
arguing.
I ultimately
found a
dichotomy of
enigmatic
middle ground
after a
hundred
futile wrestling
years.

First Day

Trace remnants linger
like faint images
floating in morning fog.
I can nearly hear
reality speak instructions
in an ancient language.
I sit before a reflecting
caldron surface,
staring at mirrored water
in a dimly lit room.

In black depth
I seek believed wisdom
within hypnotic water.
A vague image finally
beckons mind as two cobalt
eyes demand attention.
I sense another world
in that waiting caldron,
through those eyes and
because of those eyes.

I am afraid for
I fear I am delving
into something evil
best left alone.
I fear I am devil-
provoking for he seems
presently in attendance.
Devil-flirting causes
genuine fear as I follow
ancient book instructions.

Chapter II

Hesitating Time

Hums and vibrations,
like a Zen master,
teach importance and

unimportance well,
blending lifetimes with
dear yielding moments.

Clocks and Calendars

Time moves at
uneven rates,
sometimes
unnoticed and
other times with
great discernment.
Day after day,
night after night,
it carefully
blends into
years as if
having control
over betraying
clocks and
calendars.
People
pretend to
count and
make time
sensible, but
sneaky time
is best
measured by
forgettable
seasons.
Clock and
calendar
watchers are
time aware, but
even they are
oblivious to
its relentless
assault on
mind and body.

Reclusive

I lived alone
while becoming
more reclusive
year after
passing year,
finding myself as
good company and
feeling not alone or
lonely.
I saw my children
infrequently,
dated seldom and
did not cultivate
friendships.
My mind became
my best friend,
thoughts
my future and
teaching
my distraction.
I needed and
wanted little
while country
living,
seeking self and
discovering
my natural
human nature.
I remained
mostly within
myself and
shared little with
other people.

Singing In Public

I was sad
years ago
from divorce,
loneliness and
leaving kids.
I taught
myself to
play guitar,
put poetry to
music and
sing in public—
sharing was
like sweating
bullets—
I was no
entertainer for
I was too
private to
share and
too quiet to
make noise.
I quit guitar
playing and
song writing
after singing
them in public.
Ironically,
alone time,
private songs
and curative
guitar healed
my mind.

Web Site Profile

To shake off
past ideas and
find new
interests is
about keeping
life interesting.
Realizing
that one has
fewer needs,
is liberating, but
many people are
dishonest
when selling
themselves.
They fail to
point out
weaknesses,
faults and
bad habits
on a web site
and later in
conversation.
They are silently
dishonest about
certain things
wished forgotten.
But, history
beckons and
personal
attributes surface
for anyone
wishing to find
new people and
interest.

Falling In Liking

It's strange
how one
can fall
in liking
directly and
see a future
with another
quickly.

It's a
momentary,
first glance,
revealing
thing of
nature to a
receptive
person.

It's an
insightful
thing
dealing with
pretentious
time to a
spiritual
person.

Paint and Frame

Dreams
paint and frame
time awareness
between yesterday
and tomorrow.
Reality
reaches for next
thought that has
colorful season
and reason.
Time
reveals talent at
own pace and
rarely imposes
itself gently.

Brilliance
waits not on
inevitable
pensive time—for
motivation
will not be
delayed—and
paints images
in a mind
searching for
fulfillment.
Dreams
either ascend or
get lost like an
old oil painting.

Like Spring

Nature's
disposition
amazes on a
new path
walked with
awareness—
I see trees,
grass and
flowers seeking
expression,
solace and
affirmation.

Nature's
disposition
amazes eyes as
sunlight
creates shadowy
images.
I drag foot
in dusty soil
that wishes
rain.
I nearly hear
it gasp for air.

Nature's
disposition
amazes as
I wish to be
what I see,
what I feel—
I continue
walking as

rain droplets
penetrate
canopy like
tiny spirits.

Nature's
disposition
amazes and
fosters thought,
appreciation
and feelings.
My heart
reveals a
favorable
reaction as
I help to
launch spring.

Nature's
disposition
amazes as
I recognize
growth and
touch nature—
I thank Earth's
elements and
spring-like
identify with
rejuvenating
forest

Weakness

In another room
music plays,
floating near, like
sweet odor on
hot summer air,
causing thoughts of
long ago Africa,
when youth
blessed me and
own innocence
drove enthusiasm.
I now weep and
into depression
willfully drift as
purity falls.
It mixes earth with
flesh and warm
child breath.
Black souls grow,
feel and know
nearly nothing.
Inert courage
evades pain as
I ask pity and
elicit understanding
for own weakness.
I hear recorded
youthful voices sing
about a dangerous
place while here in
my safe room,
my worldly
travels haunt.

Life's Labored Energy

I used to
gaze through
far windows,
letting my world
pass at a distance
while judging
and observing
life from a safe
abiding place.

I found
sadness residing
in a life built
house without a
foundation with
tall ceiling
rooms
placed with no
loving space.

I later
boldly gazed
outside inward
past once
feared mind
barriers, and as
an old man,
realized people
can change.

I wished to
somehow engage
friends and
family, meld

life's labored
energy, with
old wisdom and
rejuvenated
intellect.

Through an
open door
I stepped,
gravitating
towards warmth
in quest of
smiling faces,
open arms and
pliant minds.

I gazed past
gathered crowd,
inside outward,
seeing a face
in night's black
near window
glass reflecting
my image and
salvaged soul.

Tomorrow Tonight

My artistic
tonight time is
smeared with
yesterday and
tomorrow
mind paint.
Intense winter
reluctance
is incapable
of painting
summer resolve.
It is as if
my split mind
has a dominate
season and
its calendar
has only
pretty pictures.
Disobedient
numbers
silently feign
movement.
I obsessively
paint one
picture with
two minds as
illustrated time
reveals little
and fails to
influence
my artful,
bi-polar essence.

Bitterness

I bitterly
complain like a
helpless leaf
crossing a
parched lawn,
pushed by a
natural,
unforgiving
Fall attitude.

My bitter mind
dredges like a
naive amphibian
blindly dragging
river mud as
unforgiving,
murky water
encumbers
thought.

My bitter soul
endures like a
resilient rock
on a transforming
mountain side,
resisting
profound forces
concerned with
progress.

I am thus an
accepting
powerless
phenomenon

being innocent,
agreeable and
pliant to old
unpretentious
influences.

Forgiveness
nourishes
my mending
mind and
faith restores
my collecting
soul to accept
intended
earthly plan.

I briefly
pretend to be
like a tolerating
mountain or an
abiding river,
but honestly
I am only a
trivial spirit
seeking heaven.

I am really
only a pushed,
helpless Fall
leaf spiritually
finding a
resting place
in mind and
soul as only
time endures.

Another Season

Frost is
near and
snow threatens.
Wind speaks
an inspiring
language.
Thoughts of
past and
future ways
tease
imagination.
Winter elegance
welcomes a
thick coat and a
warm house.
A blessed fire
burns within a
fireplace that
opens a
mind door
waiting soul
rejuvenation.
Winter's
graceful
beauty
asks that
pictures
be taken
for memory
amalgamation.
No snows,
days or
lives are
alike and

should be
embraced.
Spring
is like a
candle that
loves
darkness and
adores winter,
but acts as if a
salvation piece.
Another season,
another reason
brings life
closer to
its end and
its beginning.
Spring
engages a
natural circle
that reveals
humanity's
disposition.

Tall Trees

I slowly walk
among trees
once summer
leaf clothed,
but now
winter naked.
They brazenly
stand as if
voyeurs watching
me watch
them in fast
passing time.
Some live
particularly
well while a
few struggle.

I sense
my own life
is not much
different
than most
forest trees.
Strong ones
sky reach,
supporting a
wonderful
canopy—while
weak ones
burrow roots
into soil as
best they can for
survival space.

I want to be a
healthy, strong
tree, but
eventually
I will—as
all things do
one way or
another—face
death and
consumption.
I often sense
tree experience as
time destroys,
disease decays,
wind splits and
drought deprives.

Each season
dances over and
beneath my
would be grave.
I fear too soon
chain saws
will gnaw at
my heart and
make vital sap
painfully flow.
Yes, I am much
like a tree
growing
inside outward
until too soon
disappeared.

I understand
time will
saw and chop

me down,
plane and finish
me around,
ignite and burn
me up or
leave and scatter
me as ashes—
eventually tree or
human being
becomes either
felt fire fuel or
unacquainted
recycled rot.

I selfishly
wish to be
tomorrow's
organic filled
soil before legs
cannot walk and
eyes cannot see.
I wish to be
like one of
those staunch
tall trees,
among which
I walk,
felled,
incinerated and
ash honored.

Contrast

Bright sun
creates dark
shadows that
reveal
changing self.
Upon my face
warm youth is
lost in those
telling shadows.
I obliquely gaze
in a mirror,
examining
shadowy lines of
my cold aging
reflection.
I believe
my enlightened
soul will share
wisdom better
than a shadow, a
line or a reflection.
I pray it will be
more real than
pretentious vision.
I am yet alive
in contrasting
extremes and
pray to lay
my shadow
down before
earthly ghosts
consume it.

Rain Drops

Wondrous clouds
in atmosphere
drift near earth,
held water wishes
to soak thirsty soil.

It is a quest few
folks recognize,
failing to value
silent, invincible
Mother Nature.

Water collects in
gathering clouds,
soon rain falls
towards earth as an
apt peace offering.

Clouds empty
themselves with
assembled flair,
recycling water with
spiritual guidance.

Wondrous water
of earthly grace,
spiritually falls and
repeatedly ascends,
heavenly salvaged.

Being Different

You were a
rough,
unpolished,
poorly forged
sword.
You spent
your life
in a sheath
waiting for
some hand to
grab and
slay dragons
with you.

You sought
forgiveness for
being distinctive.

You were a
threatening,
brewing
storm.
You tried to
be peaceful
by remaining
silent and
acquiescing to
others while
fearful of own
strength and
irregularity.

Red Hues

Through my
windshield,
materializing
morning is
glorious in an
array of reds
and yellows.

It seeks
center stage,
preparing to
share God's
display of
ominous
sky explosion.

I sit front
row center,
planning
ever so warily
my future
by mind
traveling.

I call myself
gallant,
allowing spirits
to hoist
me aboard a
mystical
cosmic ship.

Spiritual Journey

A true
spiritual
journey
seeks
meld of
mind and
body with
purity that is
resilient as
eagle
feathers
and white as
angel
wings.

Chapter III

Wobbling Energy

An eager man might
sanctify strength, but
cannot by himself

carry all burdens
as a gulf cannot
provide a self-bridge.

Destruction

Destructive
pain varies
according to
whom and
what
happens, and
in what
time and
space
it transpires.
Cancer is a
destructive
personal event
while a
hurricane is a
destructive
shared event.
Now you ask
what about
heart attacks,
arthritis or
earthquakes?
Everything is
personally
relevant, but
truly there are
no small
heart attacks.
Demolition is
painful and
especially painful
if it is you
being destroyed.

Storms Scare Me

Storms
scare me,
yet I love
them.
I fear
their coming
and celebrate
their passing.

I now sit
suspiciously
watching
weather
symptoms.
Invisible
daytime
lightening
causes raucous
thunder.

I ask for
peace,
attempting
higher
courage.
Threatening
thunder and
silent
lightening
surround.

It is,
however,
rain that

seeks true
attention.
Thunder and
lightning are
only alarm
symptoms.

I must
endure
storm fear
to receive
rewards.
I must
embrace
tragedy
to experience
joy.

Storms
scare me,
yet I love
them.
I fear
their coming
and celebrate
their passing.

Compatible

I am
not worldly
compatible
when
spiritually
silent.

Beauty of
physical
prowess and
artful
movement is
astonishing—

but mental
grace and
thought
acuity is
beyond
appreciation.

I am
not worldly
compatible
when
spiritually
silent.

Retirement

Retirement
transformation
took a year.
At first
I frequently
felt like a
lazy bum,
then oddly
that feeling
dissipated.
I realized a
wonderful
unpaid job was
best for me.
I wrote
poetry and
found a
style for
expressing a
life acquired
philosophy.
Lazy bum
phrase
took on a
different
meaning, for
new leisure
brought
wisdom and
altered energy
brought
fulfillment.

Mean Rain Drops

Cold mean rain
drops pounded like
rowdy criminals—
affecting as if
I am a metal pail and
they are malicious
thought hammers.

In a world where
right and wrong
wash things and
etch headstones—
gaining stormy skies
to nurture dreams
happened to me.

I walked years
observing time as
accrued waves—
collecting thought
droplets and
placing them in
my mental pail.

Cold rain fell and
carved my headstone
with stormy verve—as
effecting thought-
droplets made a
freed criminal of
me on a clear day.

Changing

My delicate
world changed
yesterday
in moments.
Revolution
had been
threatening for
years, but
I didn't
fully notice
it coming.
Oh, I was
suspicious of
church,
money and
business.
I was
wary of
society,
politics and
law.
I yet
thought
all would
reconcile
modern
humanity
my way.
I've always
reflected on
life and how
it insisted on
adaptation.

I fell into a
depressing
pit yesterday
when someone
won and
another lost an
election.
I thought
my man
would win.
I thought
his answers for
change were
my ways for
living and
thinking, but
that was not
to be my
better future.
I surely am
sad for now
I have to greatly
adapt and
adjust to a
scary
new world.

o

My new world
is coming as
it has been for
many years.
It comes down
to someone
chiseling out

different parts and
putting them
back together to
form a
ruling coalition
loosely held
together by
fear and
empty promises.
My future is
not as shaky as
millions of
others because
I live on
solid ground.
I will
recover from
change by
changing.
I will
recover from
adaptation by
adapting.

o

I am
negative about
my country and
people seeking
happy pursuit.
It all makes
me sad about
our present and
wary about
our future.

Night Dreaming

Last night
I dreamed of
being lost
like a child,
but as an
old man, and
it was scary
for in mind
I drifted
in edifying
pending
time.

I walked
streets
barefoot as
eyes
watered,
bones
ached and
mind
rejected
need to
engage
familiarity.

I bleakly
walked
seeking self,
but with a
young
mind made
old and
worn out,

I fantasy
sampled
to be lived
life.

I sought
someone to
take me
home,
tell me
all was
going to
be alright,
instead
I woke
alone
unchanged.

There were
no dream
values or
predicted
images,
only fear
that within
me was an
old man
whose young
time was
going fast.

A Sneeze

I briefly
die when
I sneeze as
heart stops,
mind awes,
spirit seeks.

I soulfully
fly to
heaven,
gathering
data at
light speed.

I forecast
sneeze,
prepare for
exit and
pray to
heaven soar.

I focus for
moments
on cosmic
wisdom
bits seeping
mind.

Insight
vanishes
quickly so
I directly
recall, write,
reiterate.

I Cruise

On raw
silver light
I sense
flying as if a
breakaway
meteor,
time and
distance
discarding.

No existing
energy
dithers for
everything is
sweet spirit
holding and
forever
cosmic time
abiding.

I am an
existence
speck again
celestial
flying
towards a
place
I shall call
home.

Moonlight
mystically
transports
me faster

and faster
towards a
red cosmic
morning
space.

I briefly
melancholy
reminisce,
cruise
full circle,
then smile and
await another
spiritually
given way.

I am raw
silver light
eagerly
flying as if a
breakaway
meteor,
time and
distance
regarding.

Apple Essence

There is
little
life
in tree
bark,
apple
peel or
human
skin.

An outside
shell,
bag or
coating
holds
inside
essence for
survival
replication.

There is
rich
life in
tree
heart,
apple
core and
human
soul.

Short Interlude

Affairs
seem clear
when alone
while a river
fills eyes,
wind blows
hair and
life teases
mind.

Silence
screams for
attention as a
deaf world
teaches a
mind to
formulate
everything
timeless.

Energy
drives
clear wind
to ripple a
river that
contains
own end
seeking
essence.

Snow

Like passive spirits
drifting earthward,
falling before eyes,
snowflakes briefly
conquer time and
space while
floating like angels
disrupting earth.

A silent white
realm dominates and
there is no stopping
such conquering
accumulation of
infinite entities,
divine gathering and
everything changing.

Oh, how helpless
we are as nearly
weightless, but
cumulatively potent,
seemingly endless
small angels
in a few minutes
silently overwhelm.

Seeking Self

I seek myself in
blessed womb,
innocent,
unaware and
immature for
fifty-eight days.
Body then accepts
spirit while
growing aware of
true self as a
chipping away of
innocence begins.

I see myself in
retrospect as a
soul bits and
pieces collector.
I know myself
by living and
exist because of
Dale and Louise.

Look now into
my blue eyes and
see humanity
gazing back.
Look now at
my clear face and
see no wrinkled
distress or wear.
Look now at
my smile,
personality and
emerging grace.

Winter's Delay

I sought a succulent
blue grass place to
leisurely walk and
calmly think with a
mind that would
cultivate splendor.
Instead I found a
dry pasture of
dead grass and
brittle weeds where
I dragged my feet in
no more than dust.

Mother Nature at
times dithered,
forgot and
frequently changed
her natural mind.
Weeks without rain
punished everything.
It finally rained
in late September,
thus persuading
grass to be green and
full of life again.

A horse galloped
up and down
temporary
grassy hills
seeking pleasure of
extended season.
Surely I and
that horse named

Cherokee had
similar dispositions as
sun warmed our
bodies and minds.

Time and space
had no relevance,
at least for a
little while, as
walking, thinking and
enjoying life just
effortlessly happened.
My search for that
calm, splendid
place existed after
one benevolent day of
rejuvenating rain.

Fall temporarily
failed to threaten,
giving reprieve
from dryness,
failure and death.
Both Cherokee and
I enjoyed mind and
body aging delay.
We both found a
succulent, grassy
mind place to calmly
exist for a little while.

Ageless Spirit

I mind stubbed
my toe even during
successful sojourns.
Dreams became
nightmares and
plans washed to sea.
Treading water was
customary with
head barely above
likely water.

And yet, in heart
worry did not
tug at self-esteem.
Awareness taught
life authenticity.
I felt little strain
after learning that
water's true depth
was just above
my cold feet.

I needed only a
shallow creek in
which to maneuver
difficult waters.
I had childishly
let imaginary
seas create fear.
I creek danced
my ageless spirit
towards serenity.

Wilted Flowers

I timidly see
wilting flowers of
which I am
fearful.
Destruction of
constitution
now seems
more real than
imagined just a
few years
ago.
Winter is
coming and
I don't have a
coat
heavy enough to
repel anxiety.
Mind is
hot and
body cold.
Thoughts are
crazed and
attitude
depressed.
Flowers are
wilting in a
rapid drying,
hopeless time.

I am left
standing with
another season
threatening
country and

fragile life way.
What can
I do but
seek a great
horticulturalist that
shall revive
flowers and
remake gardens?
I must find a
path towards
spring.
I must find a
spiritual,
self-governing
facilitator.

Wary winds
brush
garden mind,
disturb
gathered
soul and
touch
stalwart
shoulders.
Someone
please soothe
roots.
I need help,
hope and
another
George Washington.

A Tear

I studied
rainbow colors
in a tear
harvested
from a mind.
I held it still
in gleaming
sunlight,
waiting for
my research.
I chose a
firm angle
for greater
knowledge
collecting.
In that tear
I learned
width, depth,
length.
Everything
then became
clear as
I viewed
it from
inside out.
Best of all
from that tear
I learned
love.
I shed it
for another,
not myself.

Smooth Black Time

I want to
penetrate a
spiritual world,
want to be
mischievous
only shortly.
My mind is
like a gate
to heaven,
hell or
maybe some
place between.
He whispers
my name as
reality turns
mind and
I deduce
danger near.
I fear that
I am flirting
with Satan.
His brief
invitation
evaporates.
Only smooth,
black time
remains.
I soon lose
my fiendish
link, or
is it only
imagination
I thankfully
misplace?

Empty Shirt

Humanity created me
from an artful idea,
materially wove me
into existence and
thread sewed me
together with skill.
People judiciously
bought and sold,
dirtied and washed, and
recycled and used me a
long pleasant time.
They hanger hung,
drawer folded and
thoughtlessly threw me
into a pile with other
soiled cohorts, but
mostly humanity wore,
tore and exploited me.
I was human being
filled and emptied
hundreds of times, and
finally laid threadbare
in a crumpled pile to
wait final servitude as a
lowly mechanic's rag.
I, however, was never
more proud filled as
when someone placed
me in a barrel to help
start a fire to warm
needy vagabonds.
Even an empty shirt
has soul.

Chapter IV

Swaying Dreams

Be strong and saintly
enough to be weak
and humble so as

to be a servant
to even helpless
plants and animals.

I Conjured Different Dreams

I watched
everything
from a low
mind window at
innocent six.
I watched
humanity
live life, and
own actions
while toy tractor
pretending and
daydreaming.

I drove a
real tractor when
shy eleven with
curious mind and
strong body.
I dreamed
inventive
thoughts that
flowed easily as
windblown silt
off tractor tires
while tilling soil.

I thought about
Mother's cooking,
adult toys and
playing sports with
friends when
intrepid twelve.
I thought about
inventing and

constructing with
gifted Dad, and
fast cars when
invincible sixteen.

I dreamed of
success at
everything
when I drove
those
tractors and
trucks that
advanced in
size and
strength as
I grew and
matured.

My farther
purchased a
450 Farmall
tractor in 1958.
It was a
remarkable
red painted
machine that
filled eyes and
mind with
wonder when
sure seventeen.

It impressed
me with its
three point
hydraulic hitch
that could easily
lift thousands of

awkward pounds.
I dreamed of
having one of
those amazing
red tractors
myself someday.

But when
someday came,
I didn't want to
be a farmer.
By that time
I had explored
big cities,
discovered other
opportunities and
conjured high
window dreams
beyond a farm.

I Walk Among

I walk among
hungry folks,
some disabled,
some nearly
too tired
to oppose
existence,
some too
unlucky to
get relief.

Bad habits and
lack of blessings
for many
have shattered
mind and
body.
Weak life
beginnings,
slow advances and
final evaluations
have many times
encumbered
their progress.

I wish to
touch them,
press their palm or
wipe their brow
with a spiritual
hand, but
courage and
lack of confidence
foils my humanity.

An inner voice
speaks to me,
too softly to
hear well and
too pious to
understand.

I am surely
haunted by a
belief that
time is
running out.
I silently pray,
"Oh, God
speak to me,
tell me what
to do and
let your
Holy Spirit
guide me."

I help feed
hungry folks,
but wish to
heal them with
spiritual food
rather than
garden food.
I feed myself
spiritually,
always getting
more than
I give.
I reckon that
life is
supposed to be
like that on

Earth as well as
in Heaven.

Yes, for sure
I walk among
hungry folks,
some disabled,
some nearly
too tired to
fight gravity and
some too
unlucky to
get relief.

I, however,
think that
God silently
walks with
all of us for
we are all needy
one way or
another.
Hunger is
just easier to
recognize and
understand than a
broken spirit.

Doctor

Thanks for repairing
my precious eyes and
improving sight twice,
making it possible to
write own historical
thoughts for humble,
chronological sharing.

May pain you suffer
be relieved by practiced
skills and talents, for
your own historical
thoughts and deeds
soundly remind me of
precious humility.

Reality

Sought reality
valiantly kit flies,
affected by wind,
string tether and
human control.

Ingested reality
seldom tastes
like good wine,
drank by a king
in a secure castle.

Digested reality
gives a needy man
many worries,
little kite flying and
no wine drinking.

Calm reality
creates a pearl
by siphoning and
one foot moving
by a mollusk.

God reality
is greater than a
whole life-time
accumulation of
earthly erudition.

Traversing

My heart complains
like a helpless leaf
blowing across a lawn as
Fall wind unclothes
nearly naked trees.

My mind dredges
like an amphibian
dragging black mud as
unruly water batters a
vulnerable river bank.

My soul endures
like a resilient bush
clutching dry sand as
forces transform a
bashful desert.

I am that willow tree,
creosote bush and
snail gladly being an
agreeable enigma,
experiencing life.

Wisdom nourishes
my restoring mind
while satisfying
nature's life and
death cyclic design.

Moments and Times

I've had glad and
fragrant moments
when dry wine and
hearth baked bread
soothed my soul.

I've had superb
sunrises inspire
grace and teach
time awareness
beautifully well.

I've had moments
when moral voices
curiously spoke to
my always hungry,
accumulating soul.

I've had needed and
afterward recalled
celestial support that
positively influenced
difficult moments.

In Search

I was lovingly
ignited and
reduced to
ashes, and
allowed in a
weightless
spirit to pass
from Earth.

I now wait
in transitional
material to
become again
dust to dust,
matter to matter,
earth to earth,
spirit to spirit.

I will politely
exist briefly or
forever in an
everlasting
cosmos after
union with
omnipotent
Oneness.

Life's a Train Ride

I was a fearful train
headed for disaster
in evening light with
grave weightiness.

A hundred thousands
false cargo tons in
rolling compartments
impeded my advance.

Distant station lights
warily grew brighter,
railroad tracks shown
in fictional muddle.

An engineer voice
in my bizarre mind,
softly spoke reason,
"Next station is near."

Reality focused on
screeching brakes,
slowing mind and
halting at platform.

I jump off tracks,
nervously laughed,
for anxiety had taken
me for a train ride.

Someday

Hawaiian poster
shouts while
hanging on a
silent wall.
I heed it and
gaze about to see
if others hear.

They noisily sit
drinking coffee,
talking serious
issues and
cannot see or
hear my cool
mind surfing.

They cannot
see or hear
surfers shouting,
North Shore
pipes challenging
or taste salty
sea crashing.

Mind wanders
enjoying poster
hanging on
silent wall.
I feel Hawaiian.
"Someday,"
I vow to self.

Someone Wonderful

In narrow,
soiled
mind
I am
humanity
hampered for
I cannot
think
spiritually.

I badly
wish to
run
life's race
divinely
fast and
finish
blissfully
well.

My own
acquired
flaws
prevent
success as
I sit in
vacillating
doom and
despair.

I badly
seek
insight and
wisdom, but

fear that
help is
far and
time is
short.

I humbly
ask
where and
how to
serve
fellow man
in this
distressing
quandary.

I modestly
seek
advice and
someone to
right my
course and
provide
spiritual
alternation.

I openly
seek
hope and
faith, and
believe that
someone
wonderful
will touch
my soul.

Spiritual Rain

Silent
gold rings
wear from
changing life.

Dusty
soil waits
rain from
teasing wind.

Desert
accumulates
sun during
enduring time.

Vegetation
ever wishes a
gloriously
blooming cause.

Waiting
gold rings
spiritually
reveal soul.

And soul is
manna
from recurring
heaven.

I Dream

Childhood toys,
ponies and
playing ball are
sixty years beyond
now and only
mind timepieces.
Dreams were
thorny plans that
matured into
blooming tactics, and
fantasizing was as
natural as eating,
breathing and
making love.
Difficult life
disappeared as
I got old,
big plans got
reduced to
little things like
fixing meals and
writing poems.

o

Simplicity
untangles and
bestows
understanding
to complicated
reality.
Dreams are
simple success
plans in a

world quick to
stifle joy and
pillage thought.
Time allows
watching,
questioning and
fooling life by
staying alive.

o

My father
imagined and
executed ideas.
He dreamed of
next planting and
harvesting season
even after being
hospitalized with
terminal
lung cancer.

He didn't
imagine or
plan to die in
that place, but
reality struck after
twenty-five days.
I saw and
heard retreat in
his eyes and
unspoken words.

I'm certain
he would have
rather stayed and
died at home

with his family,
making plans and
seeking dreams,
ever balancing
sweet fantasy and
bitter reality.

o

I pray to have
an effective,
dreaming
mind on my
last enigmatic
Earth day.

I meantime
think about
might be things,
while presently
making a long
bucket list.

Time eludes
reality grasp
in more ways
than one and
I can't escape
dream allure.

Fantasy will
be reality at
dying time for
I am not just
imagined in
God's plan.

Wisdom

Prudent ways
linger in
mind corners,
like droplets
waiting for
perfect cloud
sharing.
Chilly
mind winds
move notions
obliquely toward
languishing
thought
absorption.
A stormy
mind heaps
wise answers
like a tornado
lifts and spins
realized parts.
Insight is
always close
to an aware,
vacillating
mind edge.
Ideas span
like delicate
sunlight
between eclectic
conditions in a
magnificent
mental rainbow.

Blind Faith

I know my hand
moves in darkness
before my face, yet
I cannot see it and
thus have little blind
motion faith here
in my night room.

I perform natural
faith when brushing
whiskered face,
certainly knowing
my hand moves and
I confirm motion
without doubt.

I long to gain
Godly faith and
know He silently
moves about me
close as my face, and
my unworthy spirit,
mind and soul.

I fear that
I shall never have
confirmed faith and
never feel God's
presence as close as
my now black hand
to whiskered face.

Artful Dignity

I walk past a
gray weathered
wooden
barn door
hanging by
one hinge like a
broken
bird wing.
I step
over a hundred
year old
rounded
threshold where
cattle and
horses passed,
sluggishly
dragging feet.
I walk
over sparsely
scattered straw,
hoof ground
into a powdery
dirt blend that
rises beneath
my feet and
drifts onto
polished shoes.
Thick oak
feeder boards,
edge worn by
eating animals,
stand silently like
timeless caskets
waiting for

more feed,
more hay.
Large hewed
pegged beams,
fitted together
like puzzle pieces
sag overhead,
groaning as
strong winds
push and pull
against them.
Weak rusty nails
clutch to
rickety exterior
siding boards.
A unique
dirt-manure
odor fills
nostrils.
Sunlight
streams through
roof holes,
creating
dust walls of
infinite
tiny spirits
drifting together,
seeking a
rest place.
Empty stall
partitions yet
staunchly stand
tired, dirty and
stained.
Whole barn
seems to be
waiting for

more cattle,
more horses,
more attention.
I can see an
old farm house
through a
weather created,
siding
hole not big
enough to
walk through,
but wide
enough to
see through.
House is no
better off than
old exhausted
barn, or
for that matter,
old exhausted
me.
I walk through
house rooms,
recalling history.
Termites have
ruined and
made it unsafe.
My old
forgetful mind
and reminding
aching body are
similarly worn,
damaged and
dilapidated, but
we are yet here.

Waiting on Day

I am lying
motionless and
complicated,
respectfully
waiting for
arriving tomorrow.
It is four o-clock,
morning dark and
dreams are fading.
I cannot escape
sleeping futility or
grapple with
lingering
false thoughts and
possible day
predictions.

Grand ideas
yet tease
my foolish mind.
Sometimes
I want to be
Nostradamus, but
sanity will not
allow such a
crazy notion.
Ideas and
thoughts,
predictions and
hints are fading,
passing into
another
mind place.

I'm becoming
rational
again as morning
light wakes
me fully.
Gone are night
ambitions and
solutions.
Gone are
thoughts
bent on
destruction
through confusion.
I don't feel
like sleeping or
dreaming anymore.

I am standing
in front of
silver and
glass,
reflecting body,
but mind is
yet veiled,
simple and
respectful,
waiting on day.
Sunlight too
soon hurts
my eyes as
I gaze through a
window at
bright reality.

Chapter V

Abating Courage

Life's intention is
finding self in a
jungle of mind that

tangles and injures
while one discovers
own simple psyche.

Mysterious Courage

I found
courage a
mysterious
thing from
birth to
death and
inevitably
required
during a
stalwart
man's life.

I cried
alone in a
crib for
first two
weeks of
my life
with colic,
but found
courage to
defeat
suffering.

I bravely
waited for
lungs to
inhale and
exhale
again after
falling
fifteen feet
from a tree
scared and

breathless.

I wanted
to quit a
basketball
game in
high school
with a torn
ankle, but
found tape
and courage
enough to
continue.

I found
courage
enough to
not cry
most nights
when I was
first divorced,
childless and
depressed in a
cold, dirty
apartment.

I weakly
identified,
defined and
exemplified
courage
from birth
to death
with tears,
fears,
faltering
and failure.

Mystical Courage

Courage is a
simple thing
that cannot
speak or
give advice.
It waits to
be seldom
utilized
when no
other action is
available.
Courage is
required
when no one
else can
fight or
accept hurt,
no other
path is
available and
humanity
demands
assistance.
It takes
courage to
falter and
keep trying
without fear
of failure.
Courage
speaks with
humanitarian
action.

Flicker and Fade

I replaced a
light bulb
that had a
two-year
life prediction.
It lasted
three months.
I think
someone lied
to me, or did
uncertainty
exercise reality.

It now exists
in a box with
other bulbs
waiting to be
recycled.
Sometimes
I surely feel
like that
helpless
light bulb,
just trying
to enlighten.

I am trying
to remain
fairly cool
and live a
long time.
Uncertainty,
however,
often meets

reality for
vital and
trivial things.

Even people
like me can
blow like a
bulb and
be put in a
recycling box.
I could
flicker a
few times and
then slowly
fade to
uselessness.

I could,
however,
just have
one big bright
flash and
be done
in a moment.
I imagine
both ways of
dying, but
ignorantly
leave it open.

There are
many ways of
departing, but
destroying
one's own
filament is
an extreme

big flash
alternative.
I fear any big
flash choice
is surely bad.

I prefer to
slowly die
with a few
flickers and
then a slow
fade like a
light bulb,
trying to
enlighten,
remaining fairly
cool and
living long.

o

She was
born with
intrepid
expectations,
but no
predictions or
warranties.

She was
prayed to
live long,
but destiny
met actuality
and she died
too soon.

Stuck In History

I think
in continuous
unfolding
now, but
anxiously live
in precarious
history.

I flounder
in previously
collected
data as
brain collects,
mind assays,
self recalls.

I fool
myself into
believing that
I expand
present time
as historical
time dithers.

I predict
future, but
live present
based on
precarious
historical
application.

Precious Moments

There are
only a few
moments
when one
can fall
in love—a
short time to
adapt and
freely share
oneself, to
willingly and
thoughtlessly
be pure, to
understand
that passion
cultivates
honesty—for
true loving
moments
cannot be
duplicated,
only looked
upon as
retrievable
memories
never to be
lived again.

Noticed Time

I can relate
to dangerous
time passing at
given moments.
It yet evades
understanding and
provokes
thought about
accumulation.

Today time
oddly crawls
like a turtle, yet
last week it flew
like an eagle.
I see it second
by second
chopping at
my flimsy life.

I can study
segmenting
days and
months, but
cannot realize
my every lived
2,273,745,619
and counting
moments.

Emerald Grass

Spring
came early
last year and
late this year,
and both
times silent
growing
blue grass
surprised me.

It seems
to grow
precariously
healthier
and taller by
each hour
of devious
day behind
my back.

My little
lawn mower
groans and
moans
each year as
I curse a
couple of
times while
being lazy.

I, however,
cannot help
but admire
that beautiful,

emerald green
Indiana grass
I never see
other places.

Spring sun
and rain
tease it taller
and brighter,
making me
work tussle
and little
mower power
struggle.

I cannot
remember
mower
moaning or
me cursing
after all
is mowed
short, level
and beautiful.

I surely do
appreciate
Indiana
emerald grass
and think
it is a
wonderful
springtime
phenomenon.

More Time

Gaze across a
Pedestrian bridge,
Sit on a bench or
Walk river bank.
Talk humbly of
Self, but
Comfortably
Speak of easy
Simple bonds.
Talk as if
Both want a
Relationship and
Have given it
Thought.
Let something
Special happen
With little
Control over it.
Do not slow or
Change anything.
Let time
Construct a
Relationship
Without
Effort and
Do not
Conflict it.

Piranha School

Time feeds on
moments,
then hours,
days and years,
like piranha
eat flesh,
until life is
consumed.
Years pass
unnoticed,
fade without
warning and
disappear in
piranha time.

Reality is a
tainted river
serving as an
accomplice,
allowing time
to feed on
existence.
Time threatens
deep eating
of mind,
body and
soul down to
primitive
salty bone.

Red Sunset

I saw a
huge round,
red setting
sun in a
magnifying,
haze-filtered
dusk horizon.
It struck
my eyes
instantly while
turning a
corner in
my Jeep
heading west.
It appeared
intermittently
through trees
for a few
minutes and
then disappeared
in fifteen
seconds behind
interfering
dark clouds.
Its splendor
nearly took
my breath, and
I took it as a
spiritual sign
to be later
interpreted.

Songs of Today

A haunting
loud melody
used to teach
me religion
Sunday after
Sunday.
It was a
repetitive,
obnoxious
song that
didn't till mind,
grow wheat
in willing soil or
grind spiritual
grain into
sacred bread.

I now hear a
softer song
after all these
years that
sounds more
like a forgiving,
gentle wind.
It allows
cultivated
soil to turn
church into an
abundant field
that inspires
my new spiritual,
tilling mind for
feeding souls.

Time is a Phony

Time is a
phony and a
cheat that
feigns itself
to everyone.
It is a
measuring
tool that is
definite, but
consists of
an infinite
number of
elusive,
inert units.

Time is
sensed, but
not realized
in a lifetime
that normally
is between a
second and
seventy years.
Yet rational
minds often
answer quality
and length of
life with
timeless words.

Phony time
skews its
length and
width,

weight and
density,
often making
life at end
seem a brief
moment of
moot quality.

It historically
passes while
pretentiously
future waiting.
It is presently
sensed without
true awareness.
It invariably
cheats everyone
out of life with
propaganda.

Variable
earthly time
personally begins
and ends with
biased birth
and death while
Heavenly time
is everlasting
and impartial.

Time Makes Me Sad

Time
frequently
makes me
sad, for
it eternally
measures
dutiful
success and
disobedient
failure.

My heart is
touched by
time notice,
warning and
surprise, yet
I struggle
for even
momentary
emotional
expression.

I will
never have
enough time,
to give back
for blessings
received, and
my hungry
humanity
weeps for
more of it.

Time Travel

I time travel
to depart
present time,
transport at
light speed in
recalling mind,
wishing future
direction, but
only past path
is possible.

I spiritually
travel into
past to enter
future, recalling
perceptions to
recreate history and
become again
what once I was
before what
now I am.

I travel
on electrical
synapse and
silver strands,
in eternal
time and
ethereal space,
experiencing
collected soul
in apt mind.

Time, Life and I

I didn't seek
that one word
from her, yet
I did wish to
see her again.
I asked and
she said, "Yes."
I planned to
wait for further
developments,
be patient and
let relationship
develop into
friendship.
I hadn't wished
to hear that
one word for a
long time,
not sure
I ever wanted
it directed
again towards
wary me.
I, however,
changed as
we nurtured
friendship into
companionship.
Hearing that
she "loved" me
was a one
word lyric to
my melodic
ears.

Wilting

My existence
is wilting as
time aids eyes
to see truth
about getting
older and
hopefully
wiser before
I lose sight.

I look at
face and
see further
truth that
mind has
been lying
about cruel
time passing
without harm.

I look
inside at
heart beating
faster and
lungs breathing
deeper as
body works hard
at what used
to be easy.

Oh God
what is
happening
to me?

Am I falling
apart right
before my
mirrored
blue eyes?

An answer
came to mind:
no, you are
wilting like a
superb flower,
tall tree or
wheat stalk
serving God
in due time.

See past
blue eyes,
wrinkled skin,
and white hair,
see deep within
your collected
soul and
gather mirrored
wisdom.

You are that
little boy in an
advantageous
old man body.
Mindfully see a
reflected face of
original spirit
and rediscover
yourself today.

Tethered Time

Many complex things are
Actually simple and
Many simple things are
Decidedly complex.
Time for instance
Seems simple, but
It is far from simple.
It's like time is on a
String being whirled
Through space by
Some God helper.
Thing is, there are
Infinite string swingers,
Swinging an infinite
Number of strings.
Time is an array of
Complicated string webs.
A human being grasps
Only one simple time string.

o

I feel as if
on a time string
being hurled
through
space at some
scary rate by a
God helper,
swinging string
with a weird
sense of humor,
whimsically
altering time.

I began at a
pivotal point
at birth, but now
I am old and
seem to be near
fast moving
tethered end.
I am at another's
mercy and a
little scared with
little precious
time left.

o

I began life at
my personal
universe center,
time string tethered,
strong hand held.
Time moved with
centrifugal force.
I lived in an
eternal moment
of spinning time.

Its end was
far beyond my
comprehension.
I, however,
noticed time
moving faster,
going fastest
at magnificent
time string
swinging end.

I worried
someone would
tire or decide to
quit swinging.
I worried about
time string faltering.
It all got very
complicated when
my time slinger
finally let go.

I now fully
understand time.
I became a time
swinger myself.
Rest assured and
don't worry for
I will continue a
constant effort to
keep my earthly
time string steady as
long as possible.

Peace Is Coming

I confront
courage on a
new day,
fix senses,
prepare to
befriend
my mind,
soul and
spirit in
another
dimension.
My jeweled
ideas get
spoken.
I hear
another
teaching,
tears fall.
A love
aberration
surfaces.
I am
enchanted,
thoughtful,
unashamed.
Empathy is
my gate to
heaven.
I deduce
peace is
coming.
I lose fear,
gain liberation.

Chapter VI

Lurching Plans

A secretive man
seeks a place to lie,
place to stay and share

private eyes watching,
listening, placing
awkward words on paper.

Lost Days

There were many
days lost to
confusion, but
there were a
few enlightening
moments that
erased sad days,
allowing your
return to a
tolerant world.
You asked, where
are those days of
mind circling
gray clouds and
little hope of
sunshine?

It matters not
sad day place,
they are gone,
put away in a
mental book
best left alone.
There are now
joyful days that
meld together to
form a new life.
There are now
few sad days
lost while
many erasing
moments are
found.

No Better Day

Deep blue
clear water
flows slowly
past tree lined
river banks.
We pass time in
nature's wonder as
it humbly seeks
appreciation.

Small ripples
sunlight dance
while wary fish
swim near surface.
Fifteen feet deep
clear water reveals
energetic fish with
sensitive eyes and
agile appendages.

We cruise slowly
up river against a
slight breeze that
brushes faces and
tickles bare shoulders.
Our captured hair
beneath hats
wishes to be free
like teasing wind.

Everything
seems to have
soul and mind.
Our intrigued

minds and eyes
search for
slow moving, yet
agile manatee,
grass feeding.

We like them,
seek warm water,
agreeing there is
no better day than
leisurely heading
six miles up an
always enchanting
Wakulla River
in February.

Notions

Narrow opportunity
windows are frequently
evident in retrospect.
Many opportunities,
aspects and decisions
are usually a matter of
momentary chance.
Opportune times are
narrow windows that
give little time to act.
Short and tenuous time
measures itself secretly.
Circumstances must be
correct for some things
to justifiably succeed.
Life moments must be
grasped and followed with
heartfelt notions for
they appear infrequently.

Swooping Talons

Reluctance feeds
human minds
like fear feeds
rabbit ignorance
because
it seems as if
mighty God
swoops with
giant talons to
grab and
consume so
many things.
He admittedly
gives and
takes without
understanding.
Everyone knows
dangerous
talons, but
few know
fruitful
hands.
Hear not
"no,"
seek salty
shores and
steep
mountains.
Fear not time,
talons or
negative
embraces.

Seeds

Carry twelve pages,
tie a rope knot,
pour truth into a
new house cup.

Our constitution
lives everywhere while
Jefferson haunts as if
yesterday is today.

Our ovens bake,
horses carry and
hands fold as we
yet seek tomorrow.

Radical change
seeks today as a
few steps forward
challenge everything.

Dust flies where
others walk as
light reflects beyond
open windows.

Come live where
whispers historically
linger in rooms
forefathers designed.

All will hear
you call beyond
printing presses and
open windows.

All will see
stars and stripes,
courage draped over
shoulders like a flag.

Count liberty ways,
place them in a
box headed for
Washington, DC.

Tomorrow's realm
touches shoulders,
pushes backs and
rejoices restorations.

Oh, there's a
change coming,
Jefferson whispers and
argues with Adams.

Hear them in mind,
feel them in heart and
cast inspiration again
in a Liberty Bell.

Four Hours

I recall when
you were vague
about me.
Whether to
abandon or
embrace was
your dilemma.
You chose
both within a
quarter hour.

You briefly chose
him over me,
went back to
your old life and
rejected newness.
You soon
changed mind,
abandoned,
embraced and
went forward.

I won you,
received hug,
got kissed.
Circumstances
got turned
up-side-down.
You embraced
freedom and
valued calm
after storm.

You Sought Freedom

You sought
freedom like a
thirsty flower
shadow placed,
needing space.
I became a
liberating
warrior,
guide for
our shared
adventure.
We used
mutual glow
to illumine
new courses.

We gained
enthusiasm,
momentum as
you broke
stifling clay pot,
shed shadow,
became an
open-air
sun flower.
You grew in
novel ways,
liberty directed,
joy poised,
wholly loved.

Only Yesterday

I restlessly sit,
thinking that
I should
accomplish
something, for
sneaky time is
noticeably
ever fleeting.

It seems
only yesterday
I traveled to
Colorado and
last month to
Memphis.
It seems
only a few
years ago in
cold ground
I put
my friend
Steve,
only a few
years ago on
dresser top
I placed
my sweet
Kaitlyn's
ashes.

Oh, behold
time,
that silent
enemy of

life,
that savage
eater of
flesh and
bone.
I am but a
seeker of last
day living and
ignorantly
showing it.
I turn
my attention
often towards
yesterday,
melancholy
remembering,
not thinking
enough about
tomorrow
living.

I restlessly
remain sitting,
but beginning
to think about
what to do,
wishing to fool
sneaky time and
in my life
occupy more
living space.
I'm going to
change attitude,
do push-up,
curl iron,
eat whole grain.

Dolphins

I watched a
zoo dolphin
show yesterday,
subtly feeling
melancholy
creature linked.
Dolphins
performed for
rewarding fish.
I pretended
they were happy,
wishing
applause and
appreciation,
yet suspected
they preferred
freedom
like my wild
befriended
Gulf of Mexico
dolphins.
I felt sorry
and guilty for
paying to foist
degradation.

I imagined being
one of them,
performing for
applause and a
few stinky fish.
I, however, felt
not so different,
even though

food chain
higher.
I asked is
someone superior
watching and
controlling
me to perform?

o

I wish not to
relinquish
freedom for
applause and
appreciation.
I wish not to
perform for
behavior control,
welfare stuff or
political votes.
I recall
Founding Fathers
speaking and
writing about
freedom and
independence.

I now write
about liberty and
individual
rebellion against
tyranny and
coercion.
I am not a
captured creature
forced to abandon
liberty for so

called security or
social justice.
I am a free
human being,
having power
to help renew
America.
I am a natural
American man
ready to follow
Aristotle,
Jefferson and
Reagan's
philosophy.
History is
my teacher,
courage and
blessing, and
freedom
my passion.

o

I wished to
free those
dolphins, but
settled on
human beings,
while teaching
natural
principles and
sharing
Republic ideas.

Exercise

Most of what
I say and
write is a
feeble
philosophical
exercise.
Occasionally
people listen
to or read
about it.
I've gained
confidence in
my BS and
not so
embarrassed
about meager
writing skills.

I accept
my writing as
being what
it is and
don't mind
if other people
like it or not.
I am literally,
for no other
motivations,
writing books of
self-perceptive
philosophy for
memoirs and
family records.

I yet have
energy
enough to
find writing
satisfaction and
intelligence
enough to
keep mind
competent.
I exercise
brain and
body daily,
hoping to
remain
alive and
well for a
long time.

Pretentious Love

True love is
found by
searching,
learning and
getting
involved—it
may well
result from a
few or many
innocent
relations —but
most likely
it occurs from
moments of
frustration,
failure and
disappointment.

Fortunate
people get
childhood love
from parental
insight—a
little learned
romantic love
from naive
movies—but
most likely
they discover
ever lasting
true love
from a mate
who respects
opposite sex.

Cosmic-
Earth spirits
suckle adore,
seek love and
collect soul—a
love seed is
placed by
God in
every human
essence—if
for no other
reason than
purposeful
species
propagation.

Humanity
needs love
like food and
water—being
hungry,
thirsty and
unloved
is not an
option—for
humans
can only
briefly carry
spirit and
soul alone,
even a little
pretentious love
can adequately
feed a spirit.

Planning

He retired
several years
ago, but
it took him an
adjustment
year to not
feel like an
unemployed
bum.

Anxiety
faded when
writing
emerged as a
new job.
It seemed
best-laid
plans can
turn to mush
in a hurry.
He planned
all
his life and
worked
his plan
pretty well, and
without those
plans,
he would
have failed
life.
He faltered
many times and
failed a few,

but without
planning,
he could not
have later
expressed many
good, bad and
indifferent
experiences in
poetry form.

o

Oh, to future
know and
plan life with
outcome
confidence
would be like
heaven.
Remembering
personal history,
looking back and
understanding
what happened
in one's life
would be a
luxury given
only a few by
benevolent
time.

Finding Another

Many times
life
becomes
caring for
another
instead of
self.
Often
unfulfilled
plans cause
finding and
falling in love
with another.
How
many times
can one find
another
compatible
person by
accident?
Maybe
"once."
However,
when one
does find an
ideal person,
finds a
soul mate,
it is like
discovering
self and another.

When a Doctor Says

Plans get
upset in
moments.
Doctors say,
"You have a
problem."
Hopefully
someone
later says,
"You are doing
fine."
Most people
just need
recovery and
healing time.
Physical curative
cycles are
overt, but
mental healing
processes
disguise reality.
Consequently,
"doing fine"
is not always
"doing fine,"
but "having a
problem" is
nearly always,
"having a
problem."

Look Back

I look back
on spoiled
plans and
see success
remnants.
Even lost
trust caused
falling in love
with weather.

Some of
my plans,
like seasons,
faltered, but
somehow
being alive
made me feel
Spring-like
about myself.

I altered,
adapted and
recovered, and
soon forgave
myself for
using lack of
research and
bad weather
as excuses.

Gray Cavern

I allowed mind to
plan in a little
gray cavern,
watching sun burn
fog outside
my house window.
Brightness hurt
my eyes and mind.
Safety caressed
my shoulders,
held me near and
made me remember
my mother's lap.
I sat cool in
summer and
warm in winter as
some earthly plan
beyond control
tormented.
I surrendered
valor in my little
would-be
intended place.
I stayed in my little
gray mind, in
my little white
cloaked self
far away from
heat and cold.
I was happy in
my little world,
watching sun burn
fog outside myself.

Witness

Many times
I gazed at
silver clad
glass and
saw myself
wishing to feel
reality, and
not observe it
truly and
directly.

I later
looked at a
moving river,
wishing to see
swimming fish,
but saw only a
tranquil surface
cruelly staring
back at me
teaching reality.

.

I could not
avoid truth for
it was visible, but
more importantly,
as I sat calmly
for a long time,
I simultaneously
felt reality and
nirvana in heart,
mind and soul.

Both vibrated and
echoed like
melancholy flutes,
subtle drums or
lamenting violins
complementing—
shallow breathing,
slow heart beat,
calm mind and
spiritual journey.

My cosmic
awareness was
within self,
reminding that
someday all
mirrors will
shatter and
I will witness
God like a
blind eyed river.

Chapter VII

Waning Beliefs

Awe maturity
awkwardly, slowly
occurs as finite

predictable time
sways revelation
towards tomorrow.

Wondrous Euphrates

Invented
holy words
evolved as
soft ancient
moans revealed
something
new.
Babylonian
luminosity
emerged in
orderly streets,
minds and
spirits.
Judean
intellectuals
sat near
river banks as
modern
mouths spoke
skillfully.

A magnificent
society
emerged as
unleashed
humanity
assembled
in a valley
between
two rivers.
called
Mesopotamia.
A culture
through aware

minds,
souls and
spirits
got invented
near ever
flowing
Euphrates.

Whispers,
groans and
cries
yet can be
heard in
timeless
buried secrets.
Wondrous
Babylon
became a
first modern
society and
where God
made Himself
better known.
Little is
now left
except Bible
stories and a
large mound.

No Glory

Few folks
seek courage
testing.
Most would
rather
ignore its
fulfillment.
Bravery isn't
glorious
until
completed and
realized
by others
after
executed.
Courage
occurs
naively
to heroic
people.
It is a
way of
life
for a few
while most
pretend to
have it,
yet fail to
own it.
Heroes
see courage
in others.

I Understand Water

On a high
Wabash River bank
I sit watching
water flow past,
heading south
towards Evansville.
It wishes to
mingle with
Ohio River
water and then
Mississippi River
water.
Its final destination is
Gulf of Mexico
water where
all shall
mingle and
aimlessly mix
together.

I sit here as
time passes
with notice, and
with further thought.
I conclude that
water is like
my time,
passing and
moving
onward past
Evansville,
even past
notice.

I can literally
see time passing,
moving like a
river with
measurement and
speed.
I can see it
rippling, cresting and
lapping.
I listen and
it seems to speak.
I learn that
water is water and
it all speaks
same philosophy.

To understand
love and
joy is to
understand a river.
To understand a
river is to
understand
time, life and
death.
I understand
water flowing and
time passing.
I am a humble
water droplet,
enduring time.
I am part of
earthly water,
experiencing
God's
watchful eye.

Her Oak Box

I touch a
small artfully
constructed
oak box
waiting future
instructions.
I formulate
short-lived
memories
gathered by a
tainted mind.
My aging hand
continues to
sadly caress,
rub and
burnish that
wooden box
yet after
seventeen years.

It used to
sit on a
personally
built oak
five drawer
chest in
my bedroom.
I touch that
ash filled
oak box less
these days for
it now sits
out of way
on a

living room
bookshelf—
it serves as a
centerpiece of a
small shrine to
my daughter.
Sunlight
reflects not
its beauty
any more,
now placed
in dim light
far from a
window.
It, however,
provokes
wonderful
memories like
fluttering angel
wings in
my ears.
My little girl of
three and a
half years was
like a rose or a
white cloud that
shortly appeared
on Earth, then
disappeared.

Mental
pictures of
her haunt as
physical pain yet
often returns—
even though
seventeen years

have passed—
it seems like
yesterday.

I have prayed
years that
her spirit
would return
like it did
four times
soon after
her death.
I cannot
accept a final
good-bye for
my heart yet
weeps, and
doubts
gone forever
reality.
Our spiritual
meeting place is
now far away,
but that oak box
is yet close.
I stand in
hopeful prayer—
rubbing and
burnishing—
regretting when
I will have to
leave that small
oak box or
open it to scatter
ashes.

Furrowed Ideas

Natural offenses
mark earth with
mounded dunes from
expected influences.
Dunes forever
grow weeds and
hidden insecurity.
Misery nourishes
rough ideas into
smooth concepts.

Flowers always
grow somehow on
emerging dunes.
Furrowing wind of
unintended kind
bravely seeks order.
Crashing waves
vanquish stones that
inevitably produce
righteous sand.

Nature plants on
high rolling hills,
while impish sand
sends seeds to sea.
Surviving plants
seep gladness that
defeats sorrow.
Tear filled skies
spiritually inspire
bloom from stem.

Silent Strings

Little can
be said to
those for whom
a loved one
plays guitar
no more.

Aware souls
speak about
music silence
as sorrowfully
deafening
sometimes.

Grief causes
familiar
strings to not
find quiver and
frets to not
get touched.

Death explains
crafted wood's
failure to resonate
anymore from
skilled hand
manipulation.

Fractions

I have
one-half of
old strength,
fourth of
old desire and
tenth of previous
ambition.
It's strange,
however, that
I have
nine-tens of
old desire to
oddly learn.
I now seek
easier things in
which to compete.
I have
half intellect,
twice wisdom and
can achieve with
fourth effort.
I am glad to
be old for
it liberates me to
small tasks.

Young people
frequently help
me if I act
old and dumb.
They love
telling and
showing me what
they know, and

how strong
they are at
doing normal
lightweight things.
Young people
don't know much,
but are proud of
what little
they do know.

I feel young
in many ways,
believing I have a
twenty-five
year old attitude,
thus young
ignorant ways are
yet within me.
I am now
wise enough to
quickly fix or
hide my mistakes.
Oh, there is yet
energy enough
in this old
head and body
to ward off
embarrassment for
lacking nine-tens of
my life time.

Three Parts

My tough heart speaks loudly,
not like a silent, helpless leaf
blowing across a parched lawn, but
like an unruly summer wind that
threatens collaborative leafy trees.

My tough mind dredges willfully,
not like an innocent amphibian
dragging mud from a river, but
more like disobedient water
altering supple river banks.

My tough soul endures silently,
much like a resilient rock
on a mountain side or
like an unrelenting force
shifting bashful desert sand.

Toughness causes my heart,
mind and soul to speak as if a
disobedient natural force
acting like an unruly wind
threatening status-quo society.

Torn Denim Pant Knees

When I was a
little kid,
pant knees were
worn thin and
sometimes ripped.
My mother once
sewed some
knee pads
on them to
no avail.

She once bought
some pants
with knee
reinforcement
built-in.
I now
ask why
my pants are
so clean and
unsullied.

I don't have
any rips,
worn spots or
even stains
on them.
Did I play on
my knees as a
child,
fall down or
pray a lot?

It seems
maybe I
should either,
even today,
play more on
my knees or
assume that
bent knee
position for
praying.

A pair of
those jeans
yet hangs on a
barn wall
some sixty
years later.
Who nailed
those imperfect
jeans there to
jolt memory?

I can nearly
remember
what it was
like with torn
blue jean
pant knees.
There has to be
some humility
found there
somewhere.

True Sin

Guilt
beat
me and
opened
my soul.
Lightening
seared
my stormy
mind.
Sin
lowered
me from
clam to
storm,
tears to
rain,
trust to
fear.
I wished to
see angels
in a black
water caldron
created for
spiritual world
link, but
I only saw
temptation
brewing as
black
shadowy
Satan
taunted me
in a candle-
lit room.

Belief

There is much
in which to
believe and
emotionally
attach.
With this comes
hope and
faith.
To believe is to
commit to
something or
someone.
I believe
in many
things and
those beliefs
guide me
through life.
Sometimes
I call them
principles.
I have few
principles for
I might have to
go to war
over them
some day.
I dislike
fighting and
hate war, but
open beliefs
quiver in
my soul.

Resurrection

I saw a hosta
garden plant
root remnant
resurrect itself into a
beautiful plant—it
did this while in a
trash bag of saved
potting soil after
eight months without
water or sunlight.

Out of that
hope remnant,
life was renewed
through faith of
someone or
something—so
within plants,
objects, ideas or
people there is always
hope of rebirth.

Life retreats
when someone or
something
falters or
even fails—it
then celebrates
when restoration
takes place
through
faith and hope.

Resurrection
can come in
many forms to
all things—but
of course
greatest
resurrection
was Christ.
All after that
is insignificant.

So even out of a
trash bag
comes hope and
faith—and
an example of
never quitting
on life,
nature of man or
God's infinite
wisdom ways.

Emptiness

Halls remind,
rooms whimper,
walls ignore,
shadows confuse.
Big house is
nearly vacant,
sadly inaudible.

Love leaves,
soul travels,
house realizes
absence.
Talk waits,
music begs,
dancing idles.

Time passes,
music learns
to wait playing.
Life remembers
how to again
dance without
another.

Love finally
returns,
time reveals
intentions and
desires,
flaunts renewed
passions.

Love echoes
through halls

of found
conversation as
life continues,
energy flashes,
house rejoices.

Absence
inspires notions,
elicits memories,
fills past and
present with
composed
loving moments.

Halls rejoice,
rooms laugh,
walls notice,
shadows dance.
Big house is
occupied and
joyfully audible.

Family

Family arms
hold much,
rush blood,
give love and
abide needs.
Family hands
shape, mold and
generate
spirituality.
Family souls
gather, hold,
bless and
present
thanksgivings.
Even
those with
short arms,
small hands and
fragile souls
can offer
much, and
fear together
in a storm's
raging eye.

Life's Labored Energy

I used to
watch life
through windows,
letting world
pass while
distance judging.
I was a visitor
observing life's
fragility from a
safe distance.
I never found
true residence,
learning life
building without
base principles.
I placed
fancy mental
fixtures and
brilliant lighting,
but built no
comfort zone,
thought place or
reflecting area.

I later gazed
through another's
window from
outside inward,
through
once opaque
lifetime barriers
that became
transparent.
I sought to

engage family,
meld life's labored
energy with
old age joy and
touch those
loved with
calloused hands.

I lastly
stepped through
an unfastened
door, and with
reservations
sought lenient
smiles,
touches and
voices.
I gravitated
to warmth,
reached for
humanity and
embraced
benevolence.

I looked at a
near window,
saw my humble
reflected face
on black
window glass.
It displayed
my salvaged
soul like a
quality mirror.

Security is a Myth

Your smooth
skin makes
my mind wander.
I willfully bite
my mind lip for
naive thoughts
nearly speak
my hands into
intrepid action.

My lack of
self-discipline
is like weeping
willow tree fraud,
easy going and
seemingly supple,
but staunch with
unruly roots
beneath surface.

Desires reach
in willow tree
selfish fashion,
affecting
simple me in a
complex world.
My motives are
like true willow
tree water needs.

Passion is
in my thirsty,
bashful heart,
and reluctance

is mind rooted—
security is a
myth, for courage
abides not in
my passive self.

My thirsty
humanity
greatly seeks
absorption of
mutual love.
I humbly pray
for akin leaf,
branch and
root embrace.

Forgive silent
eagerness and
veiled sway as
I daringly
reach out and
wishfully seek
another to
gently share
my willowness.

Wild Nature

Nature lives
just outside
window glass.
Life seeks
food, water
and shelter
here on suburb
wooded lots.
Wild animals
seem to exist
everywhere.
Many of them
thrive freely
in preserved
environment.
Trees, bushes,
weeds and
insects
well prevail
inches from
closed doors.
Veiled nature
crawls,
jumps,
climbs and
scampers
out there—
it pollinates,
plants,
grows,
recycles and
expires
naturally
out there.

Feeding Beliefs

Dreams
feed soul
like juicy
grapes tease
oenologists—as
thoughts
feed minds
like grand
ideas intoxicate
philosophers.

Workers
follow,
plant and
harvest with
physical skills—as
visionaries
dream,
think and
evoke with
mental skills.

Minds and
bodies
manage
vineyards—as
spirits
taste wine
and souls
idealistically
get drunk
on life.

Chapter VIII

Weakening Soul

Passion like a seed,
silently waits and
seeks liberation,

remaining beneath
hard dry surface crust,
deep in soft gray loam.

Temporary Pastor

To search
for a church
is to believe
in spiritual
possibility and
share quiet
confidence
in something
greater
than self.

To pray and
recite
Holy Spirit
fruits and
show desire for
life change
is seeking
help from a
source higher
than self.

To briefly
inspire and
preach
from pencil
scribbled
notes on a
little scrap
of paper is
being larger
than self.

o

He described
an ideal
church and
people said
"amen," for
it was beyond
what most
envisioned and
surely greater
than self.

He was a
compassionate,
retired Lutheran
pastor who
no longer
wished own
church, yet
transitioned a
church greater
than self.

His intimate
wisdom of
God and
humanity
evoked
many to
follow
Jesus and
rely on more
than self.

Bandage

Calm river
near where
I warily
bank stand
is like a
bandage
available to
mend
my wounded
mind.

Sun
caresses,
breeze
brushes—and
into mind
comes
knowledge,
wisdom and
therapeutic
truth.

River heals
at water's
edge on an
anxious day
that teaches
me how to
swim and
save my life
without
getting wet.

Brief Celebration

Soul vestiges
haunt a moon lit
mystic garden—
motionless swing,
where two drank
morning coffee
sits waiting—
as muted intellect
absorbs life and
nature idles time.

He mindfully
traces face,
remembers
soft neck—
psyche smells
alluring odor—
his mind rebels,
for her recalled
influence will split
his heart further.

Dew lingers
like love letters, and
flower scents
defeat forgetting—
dare he recall a
life that once was—
in this inert garden
full of obsession,
shadows and
tearful nature.

Reality yet robs
him of
companionship—
only vestiges of
romance remain—
yet in fantasy,
as time and
space reflect,
invested garden
existence.

Oh, if sorrow,
despair and loss
were knives—
grief can throw a
man onto daggers—
he'd be mortally
cut into pieces and
laid to rest in that
moon lit garden of
recollection.

God's Finger Tip

I single cell
resided in
God's
index finger
tip.
I helped
Him touch
humanity and
with other
spiritual cells,
we created
universal
form and
function
existence.

I pray that
I shall
some day
return with
my collecting
soul full of
earthly
experiences for
His
appraisal.
Oh, I am
but one
spiritual cell,
temporarily
earthly
planted,
seemingly
trivial and

insignificant—yet
I sense
self-importance
because
I am, after
all is said and
done, a
spiritual being
created in heaven
planted in an
earthly body.
I process
with an earthly
brain and
collect
with a cosmic
mind.

I pray to
Heaven
I shall
return with
my soul suitcase
full of earthly
experiences for
God's
approval—and
again be an
index finger
tip cell for
His use.

Gritty Past

Uncertain
questions like
clapping hands
express empty
goals, like
muted voices
echo brave
thoughts.
They crush
and grind
simple life
solutions as
civilization
considers
reacting with
arrogance.

Humanity
becomes
ocean beach
boulder-
eroded sand.
Its essence
struggles to
stay alive like
salty air and
lost sunlight.
It stands
on crushed
past and
grounds
history with
open arms.

Humanity's
pulverizing
application
artfully and
surf-like
grinds simple
thoughts into
brilliant
solutions.
Liberation,
however,
prevails after
uncertainty,
erosion and
struggling
transpire.

Hostile time
eventually
emancipates
humanity to
its evolving
knees on a
cloudy beach
at dawn.
Only cosmic
ocean sound
remains, after
all is crushed
and ground,
answering
uncertain
questions.

Guitar

Nothing can
be said to
those that a
loved one
can no more
play guitar,
drink from a
beer glass
waiting
last sip or
extend arms
that can no
longer hold.

Nothing can
be said about
music silence
eccept it is
deafening and
wrong that
strings do not
quiver,
frets do not
touch and
guitar wood
no longer
resonates.

Clever hands
no longer
manipulate
string sound,
only soft
voices now

vibrate a
coffin as a
stilled human
instrument
is silent and
will not quiver
for awhile.

Music is
often paused
for a while,
put in a silent
temporary
place and
no one can
explain how
it untimely
happens or
why Earth
relinquishes
spiritual gifts.

No one in
his family
can now play
guitar at all,
but perhaps
some day
another will
play his
instrument,
causing
family and
friends to hear
legacy music.

I Am

I sincerely
believe that
my spirit is
from heaven,
my body
from Earth and
I am a living,
breathing
dichotomy.

My mind is a
tool for
processing.
My soul a
tool for
retaining.
All that is
experienced
through
brain and
body is
stored in
my soul.

After I
accomplish
life on
Earth,
I will take
my soul
back to
heaven
embedded
in my true

spiritual
self.

God
will judge
me by
earthly
exploits and
service,
made possible
by given
attributes and
blessings.

He
will judge
me by
toils and
woes
conquered,
feats and
tribulations
accomplished.

I will then
know for
sure that
my spirit is
from heaven,
my body
from Earth and
I am a living,
breathing
dichotomy.

I Shall Try to Become

I walk,
sit and
pray with
many
folks who
gather with
heart
likeness and
mind
diversity.
I eat,
talk and
think with
people as if
I've known
them all
my life and
yet they are
strangers.

I fear
fast time
will soon
swallow
music,
sermon and
Lord's
Prayer, and
I'll leave
church with
only pious
residue to
carry me
for a week.

Truthfully,
my life is
only a few
spiritual
bits and
pieces that
barely soul
stick and
slightly better
person-make.

Sadly,
one small
wrongdoing
shakes my
spiritual
residue and
I then
must walk,
pray and
replenish
belief.

Happily,
I often
shape and
form
myself into
someone
believed to
be better.
I do,
however,
feel morally
naked
even after

my Sunday
morning
redressing.

I am a
weak
Christian
and cannot
myself
build a
church with
such little
faith and
so much
baggage.

I yet
surprisingly
attempt to
follow those
who are
willing to
lead and
help me
become an
internally
composed
church
wall brick.

I Write Like Bruce

I naturally and
frequently
feel sad and
melancholy
when listening
to Bruce
Springsteen,
but often
recover from
sadness and
look forward
to a better
mood.
Somehow,
I am inspired
to wish
for a better
day and a
newer way of
thinking.
I think that
I write a
little bit
like Bruce
but in my
own manner,
I don't
put it to
musical views,
instead to
written ideas.

Like a Saint

Words
divert
thought,
thus
we live
in mouth-
speaking
rather than
in brain-
thinking.

Dialogue
distracts,
takes mind
off ideas
that grow
solutions.
Wordless
thinking
mends foolish
speaking.

Mouth speaks
guesses at
sound speed,
mind seeks
ideas at
light speed,
thus solutions
emerge from
head rather
than mouth.

My Father's Bride

My father's bride
held me close as if
I were her only—at
end of day and in
midst of night—her
favoring hands
blessed my soul and
eased my mind.
When lonely thoughts
cursed vulnerable me and
imagined fears
threatened my courage,
her strong hands—against
my face placed—were
like ancient shields of
battle field safeguards.
Her disposition like
sunlight brightened
her smiling face,
lit morning sun and
caused soft grass beneath
tender bare feet to grow.
She made my world behave
even years after her passing—
impressions pervade—and
I feel those hands
within my spirit,
protecting, soothing,
and making my world
less daunting.

Point of Light

I felt words,
like rain
on bare skin
beating and
into mind
seeping.
Words led
me onward
through a
judiciary
maze where
wilted lilies
rotted and
silent water
stank.

Questions
arose and
carried
me towards
some deep
intellectual
place.
My eyes
sought justice,
while words
languished
in stagnant
prevail.
I had no
place to go,
no one with
whom to speak.
I felt alone

in a
forsaken,
black pit.

Then above a
pinpoint of
light
beckoned.
I heard
someone say,
"Climb,"
and I did.
Light filled
eyes with
hope as
mind grabbed
at faith.
I crawled
upward.
Approving
judgment
swept over
me as
I rose
higher and
higher into
brilliant
sunlight.

I followed a
different
path
through a
different
maze where
white lilies
grew

richly and
flowing water
whispered
words kindly.

I made
decisions,
judged between
good and
evil, and
found middle
ground.
I thought with
ease and
spoke
heartfelt
words.
I swam in
reality and
became a
grower of
lilies and a
purifier of
water.

Rain Spirits

In distant
mountains,
moisture silently
hangs like an
apparition of
infinite servants
seeking nature's
dry soul and
hardened heart—
most things wait
for a summons—
they know not
their mission,
grace or power
in collective
array.

These spirits
diligently
achieve natural
events with
ageless strategy.
They erratically
fall and pour—
indirectly
shaping naïve,
unappreciative
humanity—at
times they
maliciously flow,
other times
kindly with
affecting behavior.

Disciples

A soft
spoken person
gave time to
twelve starving
people who knew
not her name or
from where
she came.
She brought
food and
medicine and
enough love for
everyone to share.
Her dress was
rumpled and a
bit soiled, but
her spirit was
clean and
soul full of
compassion.
No one treated
her special as
covert adoration
flowed within an
assemblage of
people and
twelve thankful
disciples.

Silence

My silent hands tonight
have nothing to do
for already they
washed and fed body
and wrote three poems
on uncommitted paper.

I carelessly sit in
my Lazyboy chair
letting hands be still
with no mind, need or
wish for someone to
silently kiss them.

My mood changes as
mind and heart feel
while I become well
spirited and realize that
my hands should
clasp in silent praise.

Weakest House

Brewing
black clouds
reside and drift
in my fragile
mind residence
constructed of
straw and mud,
waiting disaster.

In offspring
rearing apathy
no foundation
was poured,
no inner walls
were nailed and
no roof beams
got secured.

A few mind
windows are
cracked and
more than one
door is unhinged
as unfamiliar
beliefs intensify
looming fears.

Even secure
windows and
doors are
tainted with
vulnerability,
survival is
weak and

flaw fervor.

I believe a
storm can't
destroy me for
I possess
hope that
some ancient
hand will
avert danger.

I need a
special kind of
carpenter and
faith enough to
believe that
He will actually
reconstruct
shoddy me.

Whisper Hallelujah

She whispered
hallelujah
when you were
no longer
foolish and fell
in love with her.

He was a lucky
man when adore
became true love,
simultaneously
causing him to
listen and learn.

He was a blessed
man when humbly
holding your hand
on an autumn
leaf strewn
woodland path.

She whispered
hallelujah
when foolishly
looking into
your eyes with
discovered love.

Chapter IX

Pausing Life

Awareness is an
inner gripping thing,
expression is an

outer seeping thing,
both need inviting
places to be free.

A Lifetime Ago

I was a boy a
lifetime ago, but
it seems
only yesterday
when Daddy
taught me
how to rake a
straight windrow of
hay and form a
long sweeping
uniform corner—so
that he could
bale hay with
steady steering of a
Farmall H tractor.
He taught
me how to
plow straight and
make corn rows
perpendicular to
US 41—so
that folks
passing by
in their city
automobiles
could judge
our farming skills.
Yes, he taught
me through
farm talks,
lectures and
demonstrations how
to work straight
with artful flair.

All Those Lies

It's strange how
for twelve years
you said
you loved me.
Now you say
you never loved me
during all that
together time.
How could you
have long lived
such a lie with
convincing ways?
Foolish me
believed you.

It's strange how
I foolishly
thought all
those years that
I also loved
you and
told you so.
I don't miss you
now that
you're gone.
Maybe I also
never loved you.

It's strange how
we both thought
it best to say
we loved while
pretending to
love and

occasionally
making love.
We really
only needed
companionship or
friendship, or
maybe only a
warrior to help
each other
fight against a
world seemingly
against us.

It's strange after
all those years and
all those lies,
we really didn't even
like each other
all that much.
That pretend love
turned to near hate.
I now reflect and
future gaze with a
completely new
perspective.
I now share
unpretentious
truth with
someone
who for sure
loves me.

Coffee Can Change

I saved my change
in a small
coffee can until
it got full and
then I cashed it
in at my bank.
I fantasized about
special things
on which to
spend that money.
I felt lucky and
blessed to have
coffee can money,
even though,
it took three
years to save it.

I then thought
about those
who have no
coffee can or
any change at all.
I thought maybe
I should give
that money to
someone
who needed it
more than I.
It was extra
change to me,
but maybe
food money for
someone else.

I never
missed that
can deposited
pocket change.
It was just
heavy coins from
broken dollars
to me,
but for sure
precious food
money for
hungry folks.
My floundering
coffee can
wish tokens
became many
sustaining
soul vouchers.
My trivial
fantasy became
reality and
we smiled.

Dodger

I cared for an
old Arabian horse
named Dodger
who loved trotting
across pastures and
harvested fields at
any time for any reason
during any season.
He was bay colored,
stood fifteen
hands tall, and
moved elegantly with
remarkable ease.
He was beautiful
while also tough,
possessing great
stamina that
enabled him to
seemingly run all day.
He was fifteen
years old when
we met,
both of us were
older, wiser and
life efficient.
We had learned
what mattered in
life or at least
what seemed vital.
Life came down to
food, shelter and
companionship.

o

I rented a small
house across from
my previous residence
where my daughter
yet lived after
my separation from
her mother.
I lived in that
little farm house for
several years
after my divorce.
It was situated on
four-hundred-fifty
acres of woods,
pastures and
row crop fields.
I had plenty of
land on which to
explore nature and
easily soul search.

My youngest
daughter wanted to
take care of Dodger and
another horse that
belonged to my
friend from
whom I rented.
I had to say "yes"
when asked to
take care of them
because both
daughter and
I could not allow
another little girl to
manage them.

I did, after all,
live there and
it was convenient to
manage two horses.
My daughter loved
those horses.
We brushed, washed,
picked feet and
frequently rode them.
We called Dodger's
companion horse,
Momma, because
she was female and a
little other.

o

Dodger developed
horrible arthritis,
stopped running and
finally ended up lying
under a huge maple
shade tree that was
winter leaf naked.
He laid down
one day and
never got up.
I tried getting
him to his feet and
into a barn, but
that only made
him more miserable.
I put out hay to
eat and lay on because
snow had come
overnight.
He frequently

tried to stand, but
could not and
finally created a
bare dirt circle from
floundering in
melting snow.

I called a veterinarian
after two days for
I feared Dodger
would not rise again
even with help.
I sent my daughter
away with a friend,
intending her to
miss what was
about to happen.
Our veterinarian
arrived shortly
after she left, but
sadly his work was
not done before
she returned.
He declared
Dodger's days of
pasture running
concluded and
he had to be
euthanized.
My suspicion and
decision to send
my nine-year-old
daughter away
was correct.
I sincerely wished
her to miss
Dodger's death.

o

Dodger seemed to
recall our visitor and
did not attempt to
plead his case for
not leaving Earth.
He laid waiting as if
embracing his future.
I knelt, reassuringly
patting his head
as if it much
mattered to him,
but it mattered to
me for I loved
that old horse.
First came a
shot to relax and
comfort.
He laid still on
thawed dirt and
melted snow from
lost body heat.
I felt him relax and
seemingly gaze into
my eyes as if
saying, "I understand
what is happening and
I am ok with it."
A second shot of
chemicals put
him into eternal sleep.
I continued to
hold his head and
literally felt
life vibration leave.

I did not realize
present vibration
until it was gone.
It was like a
tiny motor was
switched off.
I wondered if
we all have a
life vibration.
For sure, Dodger's
vibration vanished.
It seemed like a
spiritual thing and
I wept a little bit
for us both.
It was a
good thing that
I said good-bye to
Dodger earlier
because his passing
was a fast thing—
one moment here,
next moment gone—
reality struck
my own mind,
body and soul
much slower.

o

My daughter came
home early and
came outside just
after Dodger passed.
She only came
out to see what was
happening, but

soon learned
Dodger's fate.
I awkwardly explained
what was happening, but
she understood
more about life and
death than me—that
is another story
told in another book—as
she took Dodger's
passing with unusual
wisdom that I had
forgotten she possessed.
She actually caused
me to understand
his passing better
by her words and
spiritual actions.

A friend of mine came
with a backhoe and
buried Dodger
beneath that
favorite shade tree
where he died.
Three inch deep
frozen soil caused
no problem when
digging and covering
his unmarked grave.

I lived there in that
little house for
another six years and
often gazed out over
that pasture,
remembering Dodger,

my Arabian friend
who loved to run.
I can yet see him
in my mind,
running that
green pasture at that
smooth Arabian gate.

o

My family will
probably not be
able to bury me
in such a wonderful
place as Dodger.
I won't have such a
wonderful place as that
big, lush maple tree.
I ask what more can
I expect from life
other than to live
like Dodger?

What greater joy
could I have other
than to figuratively run
rolling pastures and
experience my ending
under a beautiful
maple shade tree?
What more could
I ask, but to have a
wonderful God
given chemical
flow through
my veins to
quickly reach

my heart and
peacefully send
me back to heaven?

o

I wonder if people
actually know
when it is time to
leave this
temporary place.
I wonder if
I will know
when it is time and
have a peaceful journey
back home.
I hope my daughter
understands
my passing when
that day comes.
I hope she will
be there in time to
say good-bye.
I don't want to
shelter her or
any of my children
from my passing—as
I tried to shelter
my daughter from
Dodger's passing.
I want time to say
good-bye and lose
vibration with dignity.
I want to experience
my earthly motor
being switched off.

Greasy Food

I agreed to met
at a little cafe
between
our residences
on highway
two-thirty-one
where they serve
cheap greasy
food for local
consumption.

A within twelve
mile radius place
located on a
straight line
between us
is where
she changed
her mind on a
curvy line
towards reason.

Maybe she
realized that
I arrived at a
destined time in
renewed space,
looked at from
where she came and
decided another
place would be
better and safer.

Maybe she
remembered
how miserable
life was
before having
courage enough
to alter it or
maybe she just
couldn't resist
my charm.

We met at
our busy little
cafe named
R and S,
eating a
greasy burger
that never
tasted better
while suffering
heartburn.

Often people
have to take a
straight line
sojourn on an
off beaten path
to eat a little
greasy food
in order
to appreciate
good food.

Hawaii Wedding

I went to
Hawaii a
single man and
returned a
married man.
I planned
very little and
figured it out
day by day.

I completed
paper work,
found a JP, and
future wife and
I met her on
Kailua Beach.
It took about
twenty minutes to
say our vows.

We signed papers,
paid JP and
continued our
nearly unchanged
lives with ease.
It seemed
more significant
within than
outside ourselves.

It was a superb
event that
promoted few
expectations or

plans, yet it
gave promise of
tranquility to
remaining life
togetherness.

o

I recall most
everything as
if a movie
in my head.
I play images and
sounds of me in a
Hawaiian shirt
saying, "I do."
I can yet see
her in a
wedding dress
on our wave
crashing beach
with background
parasailers, and
wind and kite
surfers.
I can yet smell
salty sea and
feel wind on
my face.
I recall her
wind blown
blond hair and
contagious smile.

Like a Bee

I flit and
falter
dangerously.
It is as if
time is
honey and
I am a bee.

I fly here and
there seeking
security.
I cannot see
tomorrow's
dawn before
today's dusk.

I am a bee
storing honey
for later, but
have no idea
what time or
later will
surely bring.

I savor
honeycombs
full of what
sustains life,
for uncertain
times are
surely coming.

Like Sunlight

Truth is like
sunlight.
It is choosy for
it does not
collaborate with
just anyone,
anything or
anyplace.
It is wholly
engaging, but
bashful and
does not
seek unworthy
outcomes.
Truth,
like sunlight,
might touch
indirectly or
reflect itself
sparingly, but
it will never
pretend to be
something
it is not.
Truth is a
gift and a
blessing.
Without it,
there is
no one,
thing or
place
that can
survive.

Natural Debris

I morning woke,
looked outside and
saw a big tree top
regrettably lying in
my small backyard.
I was astonished to
see a perfectly good
treetop separated from
its yet standing trunk.
Both leafy top and
bottom were straight,
strong and healthy, but
after further inspection,
I saw a rotten center
hollowed by time and
internal disease.

How much like that
tree am I, sitting here
looking healthy with
leafy facade, but
possibly rotten inside as
outward appearance
masks my future?
How sure am I that
my trunk is not decaying,
even though limbs
appear leafy green?
How sure am I that
I am not about to get
my top removed by an
insignificant pain or
external encounter.

It took me about
three hours to saw,
dismantle, carry away and
lay that tree top among
other tree bases and
forest floor vegetation.
My treetop didn't
complain or cry a tear,
nor did its lucky
remaining trunk sob.
No one or no thing
seemed to miss those
precious missing parts
swiftly laid to rest as
natural debris or
organic material.

I wonder how many
parts could I unwillingly
contribute to society
before succumbing to
God's deadly will.
Will I, like a flawed
tree trunk, yet fit into
my civilized woods?
Other trees were glad
they were not chosen to
contributed to forest
floor debris and
future organic material.
Surely my world will be
less without a lost top or
possible felled body.

Phony Photo

A picture of me
taken long ago
rebels against time.
I am young with
shiny face,
white teeth,
clear blue eyes and
long brown hair.
I am twenty-five,
free of mean time
whippings and
beat downs.

My hair touches
defiantly broad
shoulders that
welcome future
carried burdens.
That picture
cheats time for
it allows me to
remember when
I was a very
young man
seeking truth.

Even if a mirror
reveals truth,
my mind reflects
differently and
thinks as if
yet twenty-five.
Good health and a
positive attitude

cheat pensive time,
unlike an old
pretentious photo
found in a drawer.

I fear
my health and
attitude will leave
me some day.
I pray a
childish piece or
even a bit of that
young man is yet
living in mind,
resting in soul and
working in
my true spirit.

I pray a small
piece of that
original person
will remain within
me even if
I live to
be a hundred.
My outlook is
nearly unchanged
since that deceiving
photo was taken
fifty years ago.

Straightness

Seems city and
country folks
both can easily
judge a farmer by
his soybean and
corn row
straightness.
Symmetry,
balance and
artful sense are
in a good farmer's
character.
His eye hand
coordination is
evident while
guiding a
scratching,
smoothing or
etching soil
machine.

Beautiful green
corn doesn't always
stand tall for
every farmer
who plants,
cultivates and
watches it grow.
Thousands of
stalks don't always
dot a field or
grow kernels
on a rough cob for
every man calling

himself a farmer.
There is not always
corn enough to
feed hungry folks
who need a good
farmer's gift.
Farmers care
about that
sort of thing and
love their work.

You should
notice that
wonderful crop
while driving past
in a speeding
automobile.
You should
notice those
straight rows,
those signs of a
good farmer.
You should
notice that
father teaching
his suntanned son
about life
through best
farming practices.
You should
see God at
work through
seasons and
reasons for a
man choosing
to be a farmer.

Sundial

I sit silently at
breaking dawn,
casting a
long shadow,
fixed new and
morning bright.
Time changes
everything as
day passes and
my shadow
decreases in
visible length.

My purpose
is lost as
I too soon sit
amidst gallant
numbers at
high noon.
I generate
only a small
dark mark
with no shape,
silhouette or
shadow.

I, however,
renew self
purpose by
showing order
as sun passes
towards dusk,
being again
obvious by

possessing a
tiny bit of
space with
cosmic time.

Everything
goes well on a
sunny day
while being is
effortless and
seemingly fun.
Dawn,
noon and
dusk are friends,
coming and
going as
day passes.

Everything,
depends on
brilliant
sunlight for
shadow creation.
Dumb clouds
wish glory also,
attempting to
reduce sunlight
existence and
thus cause
obligation falter.

I damn clouds,
wind and all
they conjure.
I also blame
seasons with
little sunlight.

But, I cannot
fault godly sun
for it causes
all weather.
I am useless
without God.

I can only sit
just so long
in useless,
sun-less time.
I have no greater
purpose than
making a shadow.
I am much
more than metal.
I am a miracle
time seeker and a
serving art tool.

I exist, thus
able to make a
indicator that
represents
existence.
Sunlight
allows a living
grasp of human
progress via
my primitive
shadowy mark of
cosmic time.

With and In

There can be
no faith
without doubt.
There can be
no courage
without fear.
Courage can
be found
through faith.
Spirituality can
be attained
with courage.
Life can be
conquered
in death.
Heaven can
be gained
through Jesus.

Playing Cards

God surely
dealt him
bad cards
when born.
He played
given hand and
left Earth
with another
bad hand.
However,
how much do
we know about
holy cards, and
life, death and
games played
in Heaven?

Nines and tens
just might be a
superb hand
in Heaven.
A modest hand
just might be
better than
Kings and
Aces where
God resides and
angels sing.
So maybe
his hand was not
about gaining
pious wealth
in Heaven.

How many
bad hands make a
prepared player?
Maybe life
on Earth is
truly a game and
best played with
dealt hands
while here.
Life is possibly a
constant
card game and
most folks being
weak gamblers
seeking rewards
in Heaven.

I Fear Faltering

I fear faltering is a
strong emotion that
haunts lack of courage.
When I recognize fear
from past experiences,
I see no courage,
only acts performed,
decisions made and
plans executed.

I once pulled an
old woman from a
ravine-dangling
wrecked car and
pretended it was
not dangerous.
I was just there and
courage had nothing
to do with it.

I sensed a slight
car teetering that
was substantially
precarious if
weight shifted.
I was sure weight
would not shift and
proceeded to
extract her.

I see most situations
like a teetering car for
weight often shifts.
Most folks fear

shifting weight.
I have been lucky
making decisions
concerning fear and
shifting weight.

Life seems a
continuum of
dimly lit choices
with few decision
points of light.
Life resides in a
classroom of teetering
physics lessons with
few textbooks.

Life is not an
easy nature stroll,
interrupted by a
few unpredictable
physical and
mental obstacles,
but an uphill climb
requiring nerve and
weightiness logic.

Near Panic

I thoughtfully
sit trying to
remember
something
courageously
done and
am able to
recall little.
Life silently
hands me
decisions and
choices with
seemingly
few options.

I feel
more like
coward than
hero while
vaguely
recalling fear
more than
courage, but
can't frankly
remember
physically or
mentally
acting
from either.

I've been
fearful a
few times
in life, but

all are now
mind murky.
True courage
seems
born from
tough
fear and
raised by
amiable
forgetfulness.

Valor is an
unknown
character trait
for those
who are
truly brave.
I now lay
comfortably
while
forgetting
fading residual
thoughts and
peacefully
go to sleep.

Farm House

I rented a
house on
five-hundred
acres of woods,
pastures and
corn fields.
I rented from a
friend after
my divorce.
I left my big
white house with
four front porch
pillars and
moved into a
little house with
green shutters.

I emptied
two drawers and
half a closet for
another's clothing.
We took walks
among trees,
grass and crops.
We picked, and
ate apples and
blackberries.
We often rode
two lazy horses.
We were happy
in that little country
situated house with
only five rooms.

But, I left that
place after
eight years lived.
I sought greener
pastures and a
new love with
whom to search.
A furniture mover
said, "It would
take a crowbar to
pry me away
from this place."
I pointed to
someone near,
"There's the
little crowbar."

A big Red Ball
moving truck
hauled away
my belongings and
many country
memories.
A suburb house
situated on a
three-quarter
acre lot with a
few trees
replaced
my country
house and
five-hundred
wooded acres.

Chapter X

Staggering Love

Be like a god to
vulnerable and
dependent children,

plants and animals,
but strangely you will
secretly serve them.

Apple Pie

It took
love
moments,
aligning
weeks to
answer
questions.

Both
persona
blended
quietly,
kindly like
crust and
apples.

Silence,
closeness,
respect,
action and
maturity
enabled
fusion.

Newness,
oldness,
calm and
simplicity
bonded
easily as
apple pie.

Energy to Succeed

She lovingly
inspires
my dreams,
ideas and
viewpoints,
she proofs
my prose
and poetry,
and improves
my text and
style.

She makes
sense to me
even though
I suspect
prejudice.
She yet has
energy to
help me
succeed large
as I now
work small.

There's time
for deciding
imperatives.
Nature helps
with important
things like
love, food,
and shelter
while I seek
imperatives

for others.

Nature tutors
better than
we learn and
deserves more
credit than
thinly given.
Our natural
instincts are
God given and
deserve
dense respect.

She soothes
my mind
by providing
simplicity
like a gentle
spring rain, and
fills my soul
with empathy
and concern
like a calm
summer breeze.

o

I'm liberated
by learning
that I am
unimportant.
Only others
can freely
give love,
help with
imperatives and

kindly elevate
my importance.

I wish to
feed and
shelter
myself first,
so that
I can later
help others
feed, shelter
and achieve
dreams for
themselves.

I pray to
go beyond
usefulness and
have energy to
succeed at
many things,
big or small,
like self-
breathing and
aptly thinking
until death.

Her Hand

I have seen
her hand
upon mine
many times for
one reason or
another and
paid little
attention to it
getting older,
weaker and
less dexterous—
but lately
I've noticed
her hand being
more caring and
loving as age
ascends and
time descends,
and my eyes
become weaker
and mind more
considerate.

I Could Only Laugh

I cried
when you said,
"I don't want
you anymore,"
deciding an
old life was
correct and a
familiar place
might help
you recover.

I faltered
when you to
him returned
from a hospital
room—and
I didn't know
what to do
except calmly
and awkwardly
say good-bye.

I whimpered
when you later
said, "I want to
talk"—and
I sketched a
plan for us to
live together in
my little white
green shuttered
farmhouse.

I rejoiced
when you
baked a best
ever apple pie,
trusted me with
your heart and
future mind
mending, and
agreed to stay
overnight.

I celebrated
when we sat
in a metal
swing gazing
at pastures,
cornfields and
tall trees that
created a
secretive place
full of hope.

I laughed
when a Zen
moment
taught us that
life is
simple and
our love an
introverted,
personal
thing to be
shared.

I Love Better with My Mind

I remember love
rather than
passion, for
passion comes
in seconds and
love in years
of encounter.
I realize history
better than
present, for
mind converts
collected avid
moments into
enduring love.

Endearing love
is gathered
recollections of
momentary fervor
converted into
strong passion.
I love internally
better than
outwardly and
think love better
than feel it.
I mind love
better than
body love.

Love is an
insensitive
thoughtful thing.
It is steeped,

stirred and
poured like
herbal tea,
best sipped
not gulped,
cherished and
remembered.
I show love
better than
speak love.

I am thoughtful
about thoughtless
obsessions.
I draw romantic
conclusions from
ignorance and
affecting dosages.
Forgive me for
reasoning that
joyful love
is nice, even
for a moment,
but collectively
it is amazing.

Like Spring

We walk on a
path while earthly
awareness open.
Trees are bending,
grass waving,
flowers blooming.
Nature is teaching
on a grade and
minor scale.
Shadows play,
sunlight flickers,
nature splashes.

Primary images
colorfully dart and
create wonder
unnoticed before.
In dusty soil,
wishing rain,
I drag a foot to
reveal soft dirt.
I can nearly hear
leaf covered,
dank forest floor
sigh relief.

Nature's subtle
disposition amazes.
We continue our
grand awareness
walk that causes
embrace of
conscious beauty.
We wish to be

more like what
we see and feel as
rain penetrates
forest canopy.

Each precious
rain drop is like a
tiny spirit that
can read thoughts,
feel hearts,
break through to
buried empathy.
Nature struggles
weeks without
precious water,
but we will die
after three days.

It's a start, a
launching of
spring, a
realizing time
for own growth.
Our hearts
soar with nature's
nourishment
while our minds
pierce Earth's
natural expression.

Love Murmurs

Love speaks
both
loudly and
mildly, and
sometimes
whispers, but
it is most
influential
when saying
nothing—
love listens to
what heart,
mind and
soul mutely
articulate—
then and
only then
when time
is right,
does love
murmur truth
that only
true lovers
can hear.

Mental Lowlands

A brain is
like a modest,
rightly acting
internal
muddy river,
overflowing
into mind
lowland soil,
instigating
intelligence.

A river has
no agenda,
yet is ready to
serve accepting
lowlands with
overflowing
reasoning and
intelligence to
help renew and
continue life.

Shrewdness
floods, then
seeps from an
overflowing
brain with
disparaging
thoughts that
later accept
and foster
mental growth.

A miracle
is a superb
overflowing
muddy river
converting
lowland
mental muck
into infinite
intellectual
thought.

A mental
bare footed
river edge walk
through black
clay mud
makes a thinker
realize that lowland
earth squishing
between toes has
many attributes.

My Life

You woke
verve
within and
made my life
worthwhile.
Your
hand just
in time
saved my life.
You pulled me
upward as if
I were an
encompassing
ocean wave.
Shortcomings
became assets,
weaknesses
strengths,
I a wave
remaining
viably long.
Your verve
became
my verve.
Your vastness
consumed and
made me
one with life,
like an ocean
accepts kinetic
wave energy.

Our Time

She baked homemade
apple pie life best I ever had.

She baked an
apple pie
just for me.
I was very
impressed,
wanted more.
I asked
her to live
with me,
try country
living,
be a friend.

She baked homemade
apple pie life best I ever had.

She left
her husband
with nearly
nothing, yet
maintained a
life recipe.
We soon
got to know
each other,
matched like
apples and
crust.

She baked homemade
apple pie life best I ever had.

Remember

I remember swimming together an hour this morning.
That time now seems like two days ago.
I remember spending all morning together a week ago.
Our mutual hours now seem like fast-shared moments.

I remember when you went on a three-day trip.
It now seems like a lonely week to me.
I remember a ten-day wedding trip to Hawaii.
Our honeymoon now seems like a short beach jaunt.

I remember your six serious day hospital stay.
Those life and death days now seem like a month.
I remember diverse times moving indifferently.
Our awkward occasions now seem slowly measured.

I remember spirituality depending on humility.
God now seems to watch most situations and activities.
I remember transitory Earth life as if a moment.
Our enigmatic memories now seem depended on love.

Saying Good-bye

My world is irregular and
I don't manage affairs well.
I fear saying hello is tough,
loving beyond control and
good-bye easy when young.

I am held responsible for
what happens in my life,
but I seemingly have no
control over my existence
since events and time rule.

Good-bye comes especially
hard when an old man and
someone intimate says
good-bye first with no
sympathy or empathy.

Time teaches that sweet hello is
easier than bitter good-bye,
amiable loving is tougher
than being all alone and
only gentle time passes easily.

Time and Space

She added
chocolate chip
cookies and
cinnamon rolls to
her baking list.
I pretended
to earn
sweets with
chores, and
she went
along with
my pretentions.
I love her
even more for
her indulgence.

We gave
each other
enough time and
space for
our relationship
to grow.
Most things
in life require
time and
space,
like a
flower needs
soil, rain and
sun enough
to bloom.

Touch Me

Seldom do
I dream that
I am alone,
back from
where I came,
misplaced in
ignorance and
searching for
contentment,
but when I do
dream of
such things,
I touch you and
dream of
when we were
someplace else.

If you find me
restless and
speaking of
being alone in
my dreams,
wake me,
touch me and
please say,
"I am here," and
then let me
go back to sleep
in peaceful
recollection of
strange and
weird stuff of
someplace else.

Unspoken Words

Forgive me if
I don't recognize
your silence.
It is perfectly
natural and
giving when
I need it most.

I welcome
your voice for
reassurance that
my path is
correct and
my decisions are
proper.

I mostly need
your silence
with a touch,
hug or kiss.
Forgive me if
I disregard
your silence.

I often have a
noisy mind and
silent mouth.
I, however,
hear beauty, and
loved are your
unspoken words.

Without Words

Love is silent
when touch is
greater than
breath and
romance is
without words
that confirm a
relationship.

o

I'm a man of
many words,
but they are
inadequate
when speaking,
expressing
enigmatic love.

My actions
speak louder
than hollow
words.
My intentions
influence
my mate to
believe in me.

She appreciates
my favors and
help, but
celebrates
my faithfulness,
sympathy and

empathy.

I find myself
talking less and
listening more,
judging less and
watching more as
I bestow silence.

I learned to
love by
thinking and
writing
words and
ideas that
cannot be
verbalized.

o

Love is silent
when touch is
greater than
breath and
romance is
without words
that confirm a
relationship.

Your Influence

I seek a realm
where you exist,
where flowers know
your name and
lush foliage cannot
bloom without
your command.
I seek an inner
place where you
frequently hide.

I share little with
those who
mistrust love.
You make
my world seem
dull because of
your smile, and
my heart
soiled because of
your goodness.

I am yet foolish
enough to seek a
promising place in
your world.
I believe that
I will not remain
lackluster and
unworthy forever
because of
your influence.

Chapter XI

Wavering Legacy

A self-silhouette
gracefully draws a
timid traversing

likeness on dusky
painted earthen sand
in silent sketching.

Human Instinct

I wonder if a
two-year-old
child would
instinctively
find food,
water and
shelter.
I wonder if
God has placed
enough instinct
in a small child
to survive.
Is a child as
vulnerable and
dependent as
most believe?
I fear we are
all vulnerable and
dependent from
first penetration of
egg until last
extraction of life.
It seems only a
matter of when and
how much,
we are weak,
helpless and
defenseless.
Yes, I wonder
about a child, and
at what age can
anyone be a
self-reliant entity.

I Question

Is that
moon light
in my eyes or
long ago
melancholy
memories
seeping?

Is that
gleam in
my eyes
thoughts
wishing to
escape
my mouth?

Is that
sound
regretful words
coming from
within a
shadowy
mind place?

Is that
muted warning
left from a
childhood
conscience
that speaks
judiciousness?

I Watch at a Distance

I stand warily
gazing out a
house window,
witnessing
my two children
waiting on a
school bus.
I walked them to
that near road
place and waited
several mornings.
Now they are
on their own.
I watch at a
distance, but
my heart
is with them.
They look
so small,
there waiting,
standing
together as a
big yellow bus
approaches.
I have lectured
them about
safety and danger.
It is up to
them now to
discern time and
distance of a
moving and
stopping vehicle.
I will endure

this teaching and
watching thing
many times as
they mature before
my worried eyes.
I will later
experience
many more
similar life
circumstances,
but will not be
there to watch
over them.
I will have to
trust them with
more than time and
distance in
future safety
discernment.
I will not
be there and
can only trust that
I have taught
them enough for
their safety.
I worry now and
I am only
fifty feet away.
What will it be
like later when
I am out of sight?
Oh, I will worry
about them
until I am dead
for I am a
parent for life.

Indoor Plants

I gladly water
my indoor plants
every Sunday.
I nearly hear
them whisper,
"thank you," because
it has been a
long week for them,
sitting still and
growing silently.

I suspect that
they communicate
in some natural
plant expressive way.
Sometimes I talk
to them, but
know they don't
understand me.
I, however,
suspect that
we have some
biological link.
Our life goals
are not so
different for
we all just want to
rejoice freedom, and
remain alive and
healthy another day.

One of them is
blooming,
another struggling

with a dying stem,
another growing
wildly while
trying to maintain
symmetry.
They are so
helpless that
I must
care for them,
give them what
they need and
love them.

They remind me of
young children.
Without my
benevolence and
two minutes of
time each week,
they would die.
I give them
attention, but
take pleasure.
I give them
little and
yet get much.
I am like God
to them, but
strangely,
I am their
servant.

Mind Camera

I see a small
brown-haired,
blue-eyed
skinny child
sitting on a
red painted
bench in
my green grassy
back yard.

I will never
witness this
live image
again for
time will not
stand still, but
I can make a
static photo in
my mind.

That little
three-year-old
girl with her
blond-haired
brother sitting
near is a woman
now making
mental photos of
own children.

I gaze at
my daughter
yet today and
see that small

child as if a
camera is in
my mind and
it is again
yesterday.

Colorless
time will
stand still if a
human being
works magic
with a colorful
photographic
device in an
organic mind.

Time has
no mind,
memory or
camera and
can only show
itself by
allowing a gray-
haired old man
to remember.

Finally Home

I lay rotting
on an earthen
trash bed—
wild flowers,
grass and
tree sprouts are
patient—
I struggle with
little awareness.

I, however,
remember
tall standing,
wind swaying,
leaf producing.
Terrifying
winds shook
my heart and
drained my sap.

I was called
junk wood—
something
without use or
purpose—
only now do
I seek
sympathy and
reconciliation.

I take solace
with final
recollection,
knowing that

I provided
hot summer
natural beauty,
day shade and
seed creation.

My rotting
essence seeks
earth
enrichment,
organic
substance,
purpose and
another's
beginning.

My dank
earthen bed
recognizes
my name—
time embraces
gently—
I accept
my precious
nature.

I sense
my leaves
rotting,
limbs
softening,
sap wood
dying and
heart wood
crying.

Leaf Resistance

Cumulative leaf
wind resistance of
only one tree is
considerable
energy at work.
I hear leaves
questioning
wind velocity and
tree strength as
they on limbs
wind dance.
I hear them roar
as if angry, but
I know
differently for
they are happy
with all that
glorious spring
wind, rain and
sunlight.
Leaf resistance
roar makes
me think
about silent,
natural energy
surrounding—
flowers pushing,
vines spreading,
grass reaching—
everything is
actively embracing
spring and so am
I this glorious
cyclic day.

Sprinkling Rain

I love poorly
like sprinkling rain,
seemingly valuable
yet near useless.

Adore is
surface felt,
briefly intense,
soon discarded.

For me love is
weightless drops
on my arid soul
needing a soaking.

Over and over,
pointless love
wittingly neglects
my roots.

False impressions
scorch trust,
kill expressions and
destroy bonds.

I ask mind to
let love be
like a powerful
summer deluge.

I wish love to
drench and
soak enough to
satisfy my roots.

Wrestling

I wrestle with
have and
have not,
perfection and
mediocrity,
liberal and
conservative.

I wrestle with
night and
day,
sleep and
awake,
work and
play.

I wrestle with
eating and
dieting,
fat and
skinny,
sweet and
salty.

I wrestle with
joy and
sorrow,
genius and
stupidity,
hostility and
calmness.

Concerted Way

He sought a
fretting world
with suspicion, and
with a trumpet
made music quiver,
while soul blended
yesterday with
tomorrow while
eclipsing today.

He taught
freedom and
exercised courage
while living
among
limiting lines
like a black
composed note
on white paper.

His brooding
music fused
faltering and
stumbling notes
with a melancholy
mind that
untangled and
gave insight
to sorrow.

He solo played
tortured music
on a dark stage in
streaming light,

depicting life as
mistreating,
abusing and
neglecting without
complaining.

He then raised
humanity to a
near mystical,
prevailing height
while assessing
life with Blues
in a hazy cabaret
on a tough
side of town.

He was a
spiritual man of
great character
who straddled a
crumbling line
between two
sides of life
by walking a
wizened path.

A Nod

Day seems to
wait on us to
decide to be
forever together.
It is patient and
moves as
we move,
supposedly not
influencing
our minds.
Day measures life
minute by minute
until night manages
life for a
sleeping while.
Neither day nor
night manage
time well;
both follow
it's lead,
ignorantly
progressing with
little realized
influence.
Honestly,
it is time that
is influenced
by creation and
destruction,
birth and
death.
Time is
influenced by
beginning and

ending of
everything.
To be even
more truthful,
time is waiting
on unimportant,
insignificant us.
We hold
measurement and
power of time
in our hands.
We are day and
night,
beginning and
ending.
Time only
wishes to hear
us speak
love words
before it is too late.
When moment,
hour and
day is right,
time will
nod approval or
disapproval, and
we will know
truth because
we are
time itself.
Without us
there is no
time vindication.

Don't Worry For Me Anymore

I got left
in some
cold place
without a coat.
Wind and
snow at
zero degrees
burned
my face.
I became
less and
less with
each passing
night hour.

A bitter taste
filled
my soul with
despair.
I asked,
somebody
to take
my hand,
fill me with
some warm
beastie flow.
I wanted to
get courageous
about what
was left of
my fading life.

I laid down and
didn't worry

anymore.
I heard
Bob Dylan
singing some
song about
his baby
not worrying
for him
anymore.

I soon felt
improved as
somebody
slipped a
coat over
my trembling
shoulders.
I seemed to
not belong
in that
cold place
anymore.
All I needed
was some
guidance
towards
heaven's
gate.

Vapor Trails

I wish to be
away from
this place,
this ordinary
existence.
I hitch up
cloud horses.
I mentally
mount and
ride a
jet airplane
vapor trail.

Too soon
imagination
vanishes.
I'm left with
clear sky.
My fantasies
disappear like
those vapor
trails.
I'm in reality
again with
only ideas.

Leap to Safety

I stand
on a windy
cliff edge with
cool air
soothing
my face and
heat burning
my back,
wondering if
I should
jump or not.
I ask
myself if
I have
fear
enough to
be brave.
I stand
there for
minutes
debating with
myself,
trying to muster
courage.
I can find
no good
reason to
jump or
leap into
thin air to
save
myself.

In my arms a

child is
terrified.
I soon see
tranquil
river water
sixty feet
below
through thick
smoke.
My child
asks if
we are
going to
die.
I leap
far and
wide without
further
thought, and
courage has
nothing
to do with
my resolve.
A decision
like that has
no courageous
weight when
there is only
one option;
when a
forest fire is at
back and a
deep river is at
face and fear
is between.

Other People

We dreamed of
getting married
someday with
simplicity, and
benefit of age
and wisdom.
We planned and
fulfilled
our dream by
getting married
in Hawaii on
Kailua Beach.

Our silent
acceptance and
overt gestures
kept bringing
naive us
closer together.
We then started
dreaming of
other things and
other places, but
not with
other people.

Expanding Territory

I couldn't see
past myself
when young,
but now as
an old man,
I see as
far as heaven
on a clear day.
I used to see
with pure eyes,
but now as a
wise man,
I see from
within as
deep as mind
can wander.
Life used to
move towards
but now
it moves
away from me.
God gave and
took away
while always
expanding
my territory.
I pray that
spirit and
soul's eye
can truly see
far as heaven.

Confirmed Memory

My touch
flows like a
willow tree
wind dancing,
swaying
naturally to a
wind song.

My light hand
caresses like a
willow leaf,
gliding silky
curves from
shoulder to
waiting hip.

Creek banks
guide warm
flowing verve
that mates with
cool spring
water flowing in
willow shade.

My touch
flows like a
willow tree
wind dancing,
seeking a familiar
wind song
by swayed
natural will.

Fresh and Clean

I want to remain
fresh and clean
when I grow old,
have an odor of
springtime with a
touch of fall.
Eventually, I will
crumble like a
dry leaf, but first
I want to be rain
water washed and
warm breeze dried.
I wish to hold
one concluding
scoopful of vanilla
ice cream on a
piece of apple pie.
I hope there is
plenty of soap and
water in heaven,
and someone to
place me on a
cupboard shelf.
I wish only to be
near those antique
plates that remind
me of a thousand
Sundays spent
together when
we were cohorts
serving humanity.

Conclusion

I think faltering is an integral part of life. It seems to be middle ground between success and failure. To falter is to learn. Learning is the key to success. One must apply learning from faltering in order to grow and be victorious

Failure just might be the bedrock of an eventual road to success, but faltering smooth the earthly mind and makes possible physical highway building.

The very definition of faltering contains elements of thinking and thus decision making. To pause is to stop and think. To revisit unsure circumstances is to evolve commitment and resolve.

Human beings live in momentary time, but think in historical time. Every past moment is history. History predicates the future and many times—through faltering—we make correct decisions and finally achieve success.

Freedom is a constant faltering and redefining, questioning and convincing, assessing and deciding. To be free is to falter and live on a vacillating line between success and failure. Faltering is a good thing. Freedom is a wonderful process for thoughtful progress.

Forgive me when I falter for it is a learning process that helps me "know thyself," thus putting me in a position to help others.

I embrace a new world each day with old arms and grasp my morning coffee cup with an experienced hand. I think my mind is similar to my world for it grows, mends and amends as I consciously and subconsciously age. I, however, am beginning to question whether I am hand or cup.

About the Author

Phillip sees many negatives as actual positives and without each, there can be no balance in the universe. He sees life flowing as if human beings are electrons passing through Godly conductors seeking physical balance in the universe. Each element in nature wishes to have its correct electron number and when the balance—of electrons, neutrons and protons—is interrupted through adding or subtracting electrons, it is up to each electron to find a way back home.

He thinks we are like an electron in a battery where life is jerking us around from positive to negative to create an electrical charge and potentially do some work. The only problem with the analogy is when the battery is in perfect balance—all electrons being where they belong—the battery is dead. Then again, maybe his analogy is dead on correct.

Phillip sees himself constantly out of balance and constantly trying to find electron equilibrium—perfect balance. He believes that he will eventually find perfect balance in Heaven, but until then he strives to learn about his own created elemental universe. He admittedly falters frequently in the illuminating life process. He, however, thinks that he occasionally helps maintain the universe as a thoughtful electron in the element copper.

He believes that too many people see themselves as a lone electron in the element Hydrogen—hydrogen being the lightest and simplest of all elements—and yet Hydrogen is the most abundant element in the universe. They see themselves as a simple electron trying to find a place in the simplest of all elements, and not just faltering to find stability, but also failing to find usefulness.

He thinks of himself as universally unimportant—kind of like a hydrogen electron—but individually extraordinary for he helps cause and sustain creation with other unimportant copper electrons.

Phillip thinks about many negatives things so that he can live positively. He considers what could go wrong before it happens. He falters in his mind before faltering physically. He wishes physical and/or mental faltering before ultimately failing. Of course, this is not always possible and bad things occasionally happen, but he keeps on keeping on as if that foolish electron persona will never find perfection and die.